I0800424

KIDS' DESIGN

Michelle Galindo

KIDS' DESIGN

BRAUN

Preface

We all want what's best for our children. From a very early age on, it is important to give children enough stimulus to develop their senses and their intellects. Although we know that babies do not understand us in the beginning, we nevertheless talk to them all the time. This is what allows them to eventually develop the ability to understand and speak a language. Similarly, we can shape our children's perception of aesthetics with an attractively decorated nursery, dressing them in high quality clothes, and giving them sustainable and educational toys to play with. This volume offers a selection of the most recent design products for kids covering the areas of fashion, furniture and toys.

Many children love to dress up in their mothers' or fathers' clothes and walk around in their far too big shoes. They want to imitate their parents and play 'grown up'. This also shows that children care about what they wear from a very early age on. As parents you can thus influence your child's sense of fashion. In today's world especially, it is important to teach children the values of sustainability and fair trade, by buying natural materials and unique handmade clothes. The fashion designers presented in this volume value this credo. However, children are still children and they mostly want colorful and comfortable clothes. Children's fashion designers face the challenge of reflecting the exciting and imaginative world of a child with their clothes. They achieve this by mixing fun shapes with different textures and bright colors or cool prints, all the while creating comfortable, robust and easy to care for clothes to accompany a child in day-to-day life.

Children need their own realm where they can play and be creative without anybody telling them "no" all the time. Furnishing a child's room is thus not such an easy task for parents. First of all kids' furniture needs to be functional and versatile. Ideally it can "grow" with the child, so that one does not have to buy new furniture every year. It must also be extremely robust and safe, allowing for children to climb on it, overturn it and certainly make stains on it. Children's furniture must also be pleasant to look at for the parents and fun for the kids. Furniture designers thus must come up with extremely innovative and unexpected designs to capture both parents and children. The furniture designs featured in this volume have succeeded in all three categories.

Play is an essential part of a child's education. By playing children discover the world and enrich it with their imagination. As parents it is important to support a child's play as much as possible with innovative toys, which challenge the child and spur its creativity. The designs featured in this chapter encourage children's creativity, while also helping them to develop their cognitive, motor, social and emotional skills. The designers also greatly value sustainable materials which are safe for kids. In this respect one can observe a 'back to the roots' trend in the new designs, where wood and cardboard are the new plastic. The design of the toys is often very simple but still ingenious, leaving more space for the child's imagination.

"Imagination is more important than knowledge. For knowledge is limited to all we now know and understand, while imagination embraces the entire world, and all there ever will be to know and understand." Albert Einstein

The original and ingenious designs presented in this book will reach the inner child within us all.

Home & Decor

When you have kids, you must be prepared for the veritable menagerie of strange, noisy, colorful and fluffy toys that will descend upon you. The situation at home isn't entirely hopeless though: some designers have created furniture, which is a delight not only for kids, but for their parents too. Today, furniture designers from all across the globe are exploring the world of children, creating contemporary pieces with sleek lines and bold designs, transforming any children's room into a wonderland where they will happily sleep and play. Kids' tables and chairs are not just for dining and sitting and beds are not just for sleeping. Children push the boundaries of the furniture's everyday use and mix the sites for their various activities.

Every child needs a place to stow belongings. A space for their art supplies, books, toys, and all kinds of treasures they want to save. Anyone who has kids knows that the more storage space you can get, the better. One of the most important characteristics of children's furniture is that it can "grow" with your child and sometimes change the function. For example cribs can be turned into beds or dressers into desks. The clever designs allow children to play independently, be responsible, and tidy up after themselves. No heavy lid will trap your child's fingers and perfect angles will make it easy to find the toy they want to play with. At the same time the design aesthetics meet modern day family needs. Little tables, chairs, dressers

HOME &

and beds were never so stylish, improvisational and playful at once.

One of the greatest perks of being a parent is that you get to be a kid all over again while raising your own, so you'll get to enjoy the designs as well. The lovely *Come and Draw Table* by Tian Tang Design Studio is not only an artistic drawing space, but also a special storage for your kids' precious artwork and memories. The tabletop is made out of hundreds stacked, round and colorful sheets of paper. There's no more need to worry about your toddler's destructive side with a Pete Oyler *Rip + Tatter Chair*. Designed for children aged two to five, the lightweight seats made of industrial cardboard encourage boisterous play, without you worrying about the cost. Disposable culture embodied in a piece of furniture. Bedtime has never been so easy with Ridder & Clown's *Bedtimestories*. *Bedtimestories* is a cool, interactive storytelling backdrop that doubles as a child's bed. It serves as a perfect, impromptu puppet stage, while the blanket can become a tent, a magic carpet, a patch of grass or whatever you need.

DECOR

Stokke Flexi Bath

Stokke Flexi Bath has been designed to fold flat and once opened the water pressure will expand it to the correct size. A non-slip base and a well-sealed plug prevent water from leaking out during fun bath times. After a leisurely bath, fold it together and stow it away under the bed, in a closet, or against the wall. This bath is perfect for travelling, as it will easily fit inside a suitcase. After your child has outgrown the bath it can serve as a toy box, laundry basket or mini paddling pool.

DESIGNERS: Peter Sommer and Niels Peter Estrup with VE2
PRODUCERS: STOKKE
YEAR OF DEVELOPMENT: 2006
MAIN MATERIALS: polypropylen, thermoplastic elastomer

PHOTOS: COURTESY OF THE DESIGNERS

All Lovely Stüff

The practical, charming designs from All Lovely Stüff cannot fail to brighten every child's day! Every product is designed and manufactured with loving care, inspiring the same love and affection from the lucky owner.

Loveliness is at the heart of All Lovely Stüff's ethos - their products are developed and sourced to be useful, high quality and ethically responsible.

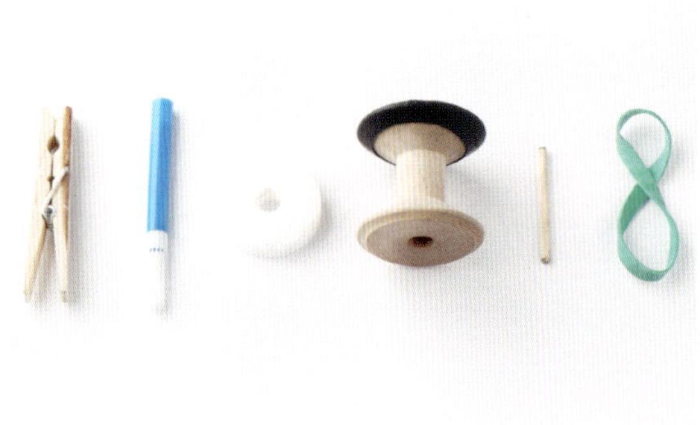

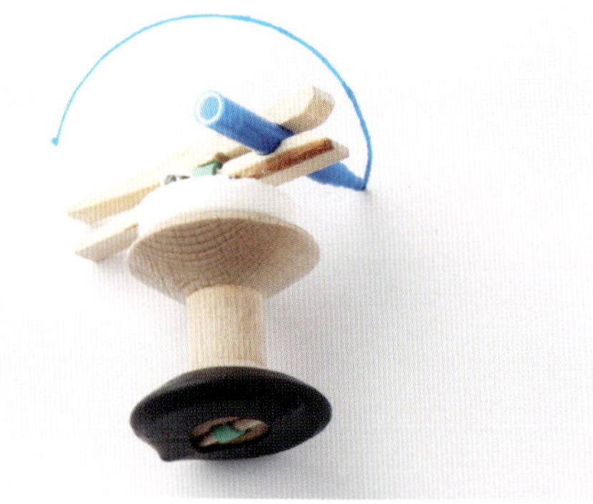

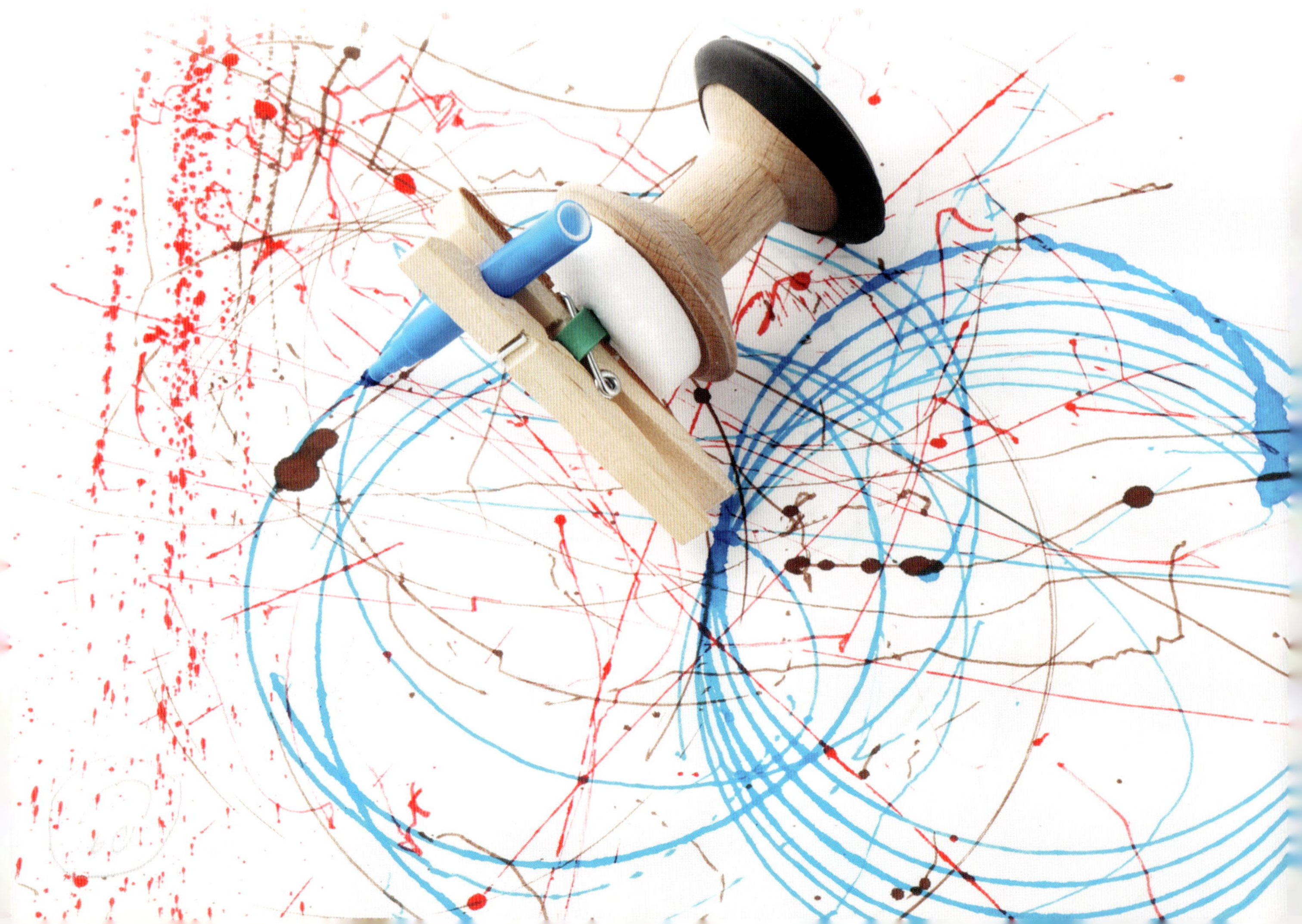

DESIGNERS: All Lovely Stüff (United Kingdom)
PRODUCTS: Drawing Machine, Animals of Whittling, Flavoured Doughnuts, Moose on The Loose
MAIN MATERIALS: beech wood

PHOTOS: COURTESY OF THE DESIGNERS

Vintage Furniture

The furniture of the French boutique l'Atelier du Petit Parc is mostly 1950s and 1960s original vintage. The pieces are collected and carefully restored at the atelier, which places great value on preserving their original authenticity. Every piece is an individual item with its own story to tell.

Design: L'Atelier du Petit Parc

DESIGNERS: L'Atelier du Petit Parc
YEAR OF DEVELOPMENT: 2010
MAIN MATERIALS: rattan

PHOTOS: MURIEL ÉVEILLÉ

Bricolo

Bricolo Chair is designed for children. It is inspired by the traditional wood and plastic "shape fitting" for children. Assembling becomes a game and children become craftsmen or new designers. The tools and wedges that are needed to assemble the chair are part of the seating area. When they are used they leave a cool cutout shape behind. When the chair is not assembled it can fit into a flat package. Little handymen will love to assemble the chair over and over again, while other kids may simply enjoy sitting on it.

DESIGNERS: jpbd / Jean-Philippe Bonzon (Switzerland)
MAIN MATERIALS: multiplex wood

PHOTOS: JPBD

Midi and Mini Stool, Mini Table for One

Weamo furniture is fun but functional, hardwearing yet ergonomically sound. The product range contains furniture, which is finished with child friendly hardwax oil showing off the natural beauty of the birch core, perfectly fitting in any room of the house. Each Weamo product is finished in a colored laminate or with child-friendly hardwax oil that's easy to clean and keeps signs of wear to a minimum. The pieces come in bright colors with divine names such as Strawberry Sundae (red), Sunflower (yellow) and Peapod (green) or the more subtle classic colors of Clotted Cream, Chocolate Brownie and Ginger Snap. The Mini collection suits children up to three years old while the Midi collection is designed for kids from three upwards.

DESIGNERS: Weamo / Richard James Wearmouth
(United Kingdom)
MAIN MATERIALS: birch plywood

PHOTOS: COURTESY OF THE DESIGNERS

Favourite Things Pendant Lamp

This inventive design will be the delight of any child! Simply select a few treasured items, arrange them inside the shade of this playful pendant lamp, switch it on and voila! Designed by the Stockholm-based design company Chen Karlsson and exhibited at the Stockholm Furniture Fair, the Favourite Things Lamp is both a functional light and a stage to tell old, new and ever-changing stories.

DESIGNERS: Chen Karlsson (Sweden)
YEAR OF DEVELOPMENT: 2010
MAIN MATERIALS: polypropylene

PHOTOS: OLIVIA JECZMYK

Carbon Cradle

The carbon cradle is a marriage between high-tech material and craftsmanship. It is a unique basket work in carbon strapped with leather and a cosy cotton interior. Softness, lightness and robustness come together. Like a protective cocoon, the carbon cradle remembers the traditional Moses basket respecting its identity. This cradle is ideal for babies under six months and its light weight of only three kilos is a relief for parents.

DESIGNERS: Luc Swen / Julien Bernard (Switzerland)
MAIN MATERIALS: carbon, leather, cotton

PHOTOS: MICHEL BONVIN ECAL 2009

FLORAintheSKY

FLORAintheSKY is a truly innovative piece of design with cotton strings holding the structure together at the corners. This birch wood bunk bed has been created at a shorter height than most bunk beds (135 cm tall) making it convenient for bedrooms with low ceilings or lofts.

Cleverly designed, the FLORAintheSKY lower bunk can be folded to help conserve space or to make a cozy corner, which your children will love playing in. Or why not add an extra mattress to quickly turn this into a second bed.

Design: perludi

DESIGNERS: perludi / Thomas Maitz (Austria)
YEAR OF DEVELOPMENT: 2012
MAIN MATERIALS: birch plywood

PHOTOS: MARTIN PABIS

Bienvenida Mini Desk

This stunning mini desk is ideal for both pre-school and school aged children, as a space to play and be creative, or a surface on which to read and write. A large space below the desktop allows for easy storage of toys and books, while its stackable system permits to use the storage space and the desktop independently. The natural Patagonian wood combines perfectly with white, grey, vintage pink or saffron lacquer to create a fabulous aesthetic finish.

DESIGNERS: Krethaus
YEAR OF DEVELOPMENT: 2013
MAIN MATERIALS: Patagonian wood

**Design:
Krethaus**

PHOTOS: VICTORIA EGURZA

Merlin 3 Drawer Dresser, Mini Library, Toy Store

The three key principals of oeuf are: quality, practicality and function. The Merlin 3 Drawer Dresser offers three deep drawers providing plenty of storage space. The modern and clean lines make this dresser a piece that looks good in any bedroom or nursery. The oeuf Mini Library and Toy Store offer stylish and practical storage for children's rooms. Children will love its fun design and easy-to-reach height. Parents will love its sleek contemporary looks and sturdy construction. All furniture is sustainably manufactured in Europe.

DESIGNERS: oeuf
MAIN MATERIALS: birch plywood, MDF

PHOTOS: COURTESY OF THE DESIGNERS

Made 2 Measure Kids Growstick

Made 2 Measure is the creative and easy way of noticing and recording your child's growth: Donkey Products presents an idea that has been inspired by a conventional yardstick with their Made 2 Measure Kids Growstick. The growing process is easily marked on the growstick. Small pictograms and the colorful design ensure entertainment, while your door frames are spared. Simply fold it and it can be taken everywhere.

DESIGNERS: Donkey Products /
Florian Berger (Germany)
MAIN MATERIALS: beech wood, brass rivet,
plastic clip

PHOTOS: COURTESY OF THE DESIGNERS

Deskhouse

The Deskhouse is the perfect table to show your child the joy of reading, drawing and sharing. Smart and trendy, an art desk and a playhouse, super-sturdy and easy to clean. It's the ideal drafting desk for art activities as well as a place for kids to play "house" and hide out. Made of eco-friendly solid oak in a contemporary design, this piece easily fits into any living room or kitchen.

Design: Ninetonine

DESIGNERS: Ninetonine /
Alberto Marcos (Spain)
MAIN MATERIALS: solid oak, MCC
with ply veneer

PHOTOS: COURTESY OF THE DESIGNERS

The Royal Guardsman

This delightful and highly collectible hand-painted wooden soldier is one of a series of Danish Royal Guards; other models include a guard with a rifle, and a guard with a flag of Denmark. In sturdy and overall good condition they show minimal paint wear to some edges.

The arms and legs are moveable. Kay Bojesen created a treasured and beloved character that appeals to the child within us all!

DESIGNERS: Kay Bojesen (Denmark)
PRODUCERS: Rosendahl Design Group
YEAR OF DEVELOPMENT: 1942
MAIN MATERIALS: beech wood

PHOTOS: COURTESY OF THE DESIGNERS

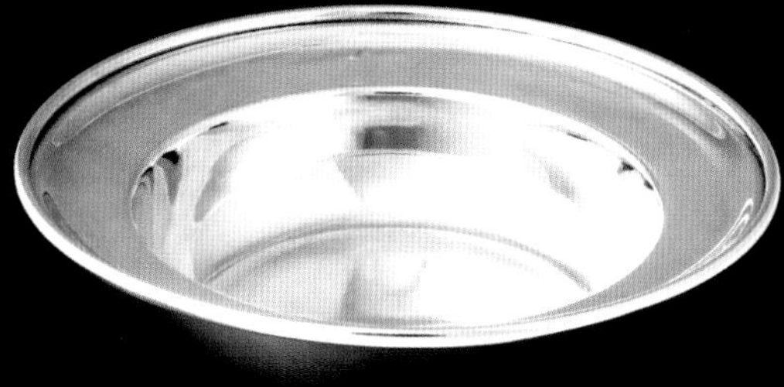

Grand Prix

As a trained silversmith, Kay Bojesen designed many pieces of silverware, among which there are also several pieces for children. In line with his classic, sleek design the set follows a soft, round and pure look. The design underlines the purpose for eating, and makes the cutlery easy to handle for children. Kay Bojesen's series received its name after winning 1st price "Grand Prix", at the World Exhibition in Milan in 1951. Once purchased, this timeless design is a piece that will turn into a family heirloom.

DESIGNERS: Kay Bojesen
YEAR OF DEVELOPMENT: 1930s (silver), 1950s (stainless steel)
MAIN MATERIALS: silver, stainless steel

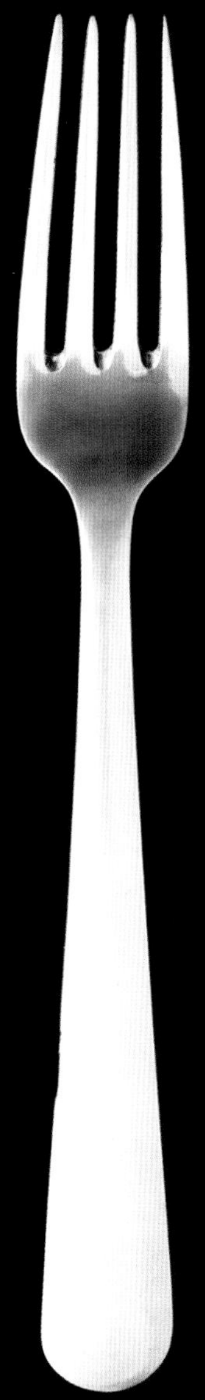

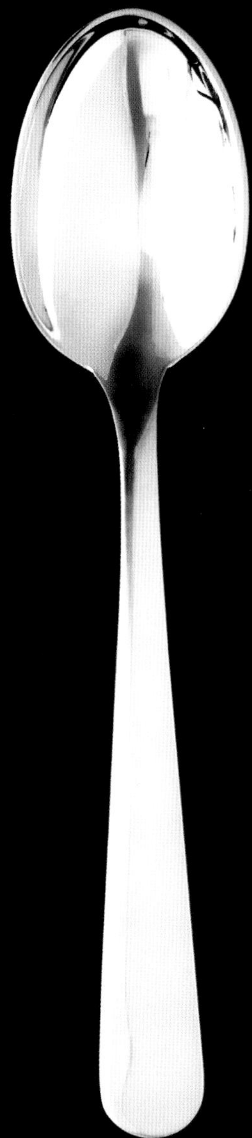

PHOTOS: SUSANNE BOJESEN ROSENQVIST

Rocky Children's Bed

No matter how you twist and turn - Rocky is a 4-in-1 furniture with long usability. It adapts to the growth and needs of the active child. At first it's both, a cradle for baby and a rocking-chair for parents, combined into one. As the child grows the cradle can be rotated 180° and turns into a children's bed with a length of 140 cm. You can use the bedrail as a boundary for better safety.

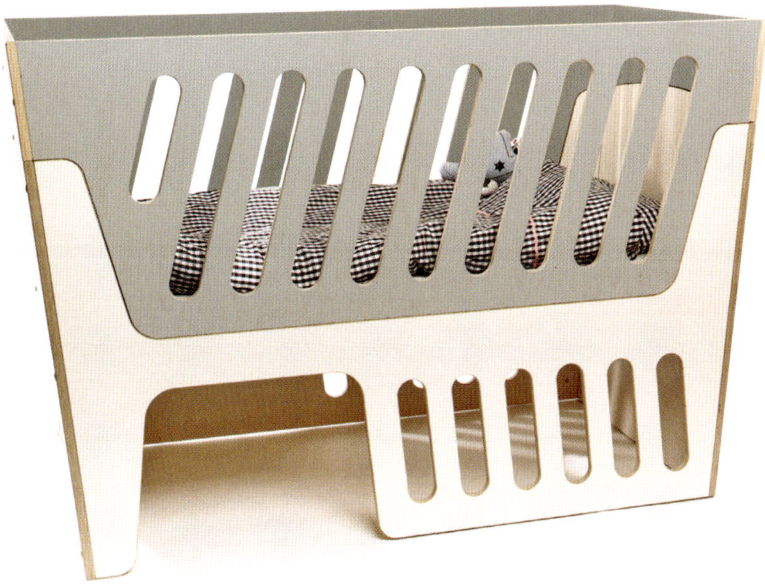

Design: Jäll & Tofta

DESIGNERS: Jäll & Tofta / Sina Gwosdzik & Jakob Dannenfeldt (Germany)
MAIN MATERIALS: coated plywood

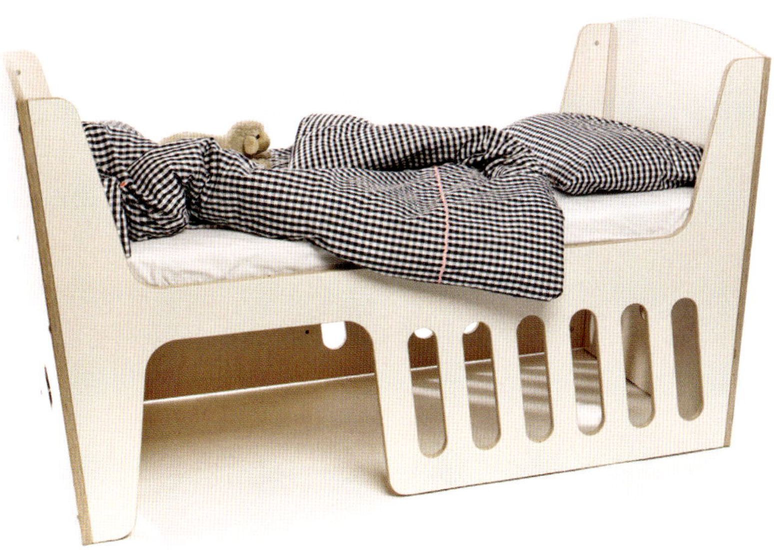

PHOTOS: COURTESY OF THE DESIGNERS

KENNO Chair

The KENNO chair is made of new kind of recycled cardboard. The sturdy yet lightweight material can be re-recycled as paper. Water-based adhesives are used to create its sandwich construction. The material has an appealing feel of warmth and lightness, and it is durable and versatile. KENNO series consist of three items: two chairs and a stool. The KENNO small (S) chair is perfect for children as it can be personalized by painting or drawing on the surface and then discarded when the child has outgrown it.

Design:
Järvi & Ruoho

DESIGNERS: Järvi & Ruoho / Heikki Ruoho (Finland)
YEAR OF DEVELOPMENT: 2011
MAIN MATERIALS: cardboard

PHOTOS: KALLE KATAILA

Rip + Tatter Chair

One thing's for sure – there's no need to worry about your toddler's destructive side with a Pete Oyler Rip + Tatter Chair. Designed for children aged two to five, the lightweight perches made of industrial cardboard encourage boisterous play, without you worrying about the cost. The chair is a cool and modern alternative to high-end, designer furniture. Disposable culture embodied in one piece of furniture. Your child outgrows it or rips it to shreds? Simply bring it out with the recycling.

Design: Pete Oyler

DESIGNERS: Pete Oyler
for Assembly Design (USA)
YEAR OF DEVELOPMENT: 2011
MAIN MATERIALS: cardboard

PHOTOS: COURTESY OF THE DESIGNERS

Constantin

The Constantin rocker invites your child to climb aboard and get rockin' and encourages exploration and creativity. This eco-friendly rocker is made with birch plywood and covered in 100% wool. The Constantin rocker practically begs kids to get moving, promotes motor skills and helps kids to develop a good sense of balance – while Constantin's individually placed hook-and-loop shapes allow kids to discover new fantasy worlds and promote imaginative play.

DESIGNERS: perludi / Thomas Maitz and Martin Pabis (Austria)
YEAR OF DEVELOPMENT: 2010
MAIN MATERIALS: birch plywood, loden (100% wool)

Design: perludi

PHOTOS: MARTIN PABIS

Caravan Crib, Divan and Dresser

The timeless classic furniture of the Caravan series looks fabulous in any contemporary space. Crib, Divan and Dresser are available in six colors. You can choose the best finish to complement your individual decor and delight your child with their favorite color. All pieces meet modern parents' needs: safety, functionality, great design, domestically made and green. The items are fully sustainable and made from the highest quality, solid European maple and with 100% non-toxic materials and finishes, while they have a dynamic and clean look.

Design: Kalon Studios

DESIGNERS: Kalon Studios (USA / Germany)
MAIN MATERIALS: 100% solid FSC certified maple

PHOTOS: COURTESY OF THE DISIGNERS

Pauli

"perludi" means playful. This Austrian company makes first quality children's furniture that definitely meets their expectations as well as their parents'. Creativity, safety, ecology and pedagogy are the motto of perludi. Pauli, a seat and shelve at the same time, is a multi-talent piece of furniture in its design and its technical aspects. Two Paulis will make a rectangle shelving system, since its back and seat are complementary, creating a harmonious piece of furniture.

Design: perludi

DESIGNERS: perludi / Thomas Maitz (Austria)
MAIN MATERIALS: solid spruce wood, variable with loden (100% wool)

PHOTO: MARTIN PABIS

The Wave

From the newly founded Danish company UTZONKids comes the Wave - an exquisitely crafted, dynamically designed chair. The Wave was inspired by the simplicity that characterizes Danish design and the close relationship that Danes have with the sea. A maple timber frame and a choice of premium textiles or leather ensure the lounge chair is a long-lasting thing of beauty. The striped upholstery (fabric designed by Paul Smith for Maharam) and the contemporary black and white Sigge pattern stand out in their collection.

DESIGNERS: UTZONKids / Maiken Utzon Harris and Christopher Harris (Denmark)
YEAR OF DEVELOPMENT: 2012
MAIN MATERIALS: maple / walnut wood and wool / leather

Design: UTZONKids

PHOTOS: COURTESY OF THE DESIGNERS

The Amsterdam Cabinet Collection

Winner of the 2010 Prix Découverte at Maison&Objet, Paris, the Amsterdam Cabinet Collection from Kast van een Huis has been charming families for several years already. Inspired by the unique architecture of 17th century Amsterdam canal houses, these multifunctional storage cabinets are also beautiful items of furniture. The timeless pieces can be used for multiple purposes and will complement any interior decor. Whether used for storing clothes, toys or books, these cabinets bring a unique and joyful character to any space.

DESIGNERS: Kast van een Huis / Marie-Louise Groot Kormelink (The Netherlands)
MAIN MATERIALS: MDF, ecological varnish finishing

**Design:
Kast van een Huis**

PHOTOS: COURTESY OF THE DESIGNERS

by KlipKlap Kids Chair

by KlipKlap is a genius mattress that can be folded in different ways so that a newborn can safely lie on a warm and soft place, a baby can play and turn around on a big soft mat, and a toddler can sit in a nice chair. You can also fold the mattress in a way that a little crawler can climb up the foamy "steps". When the children are big enough to have sleepovers they can simply unfold the mattress to make an extra bed. And to top it off - it's one very stylish-looking piece of furniture.

Design: by KlipKlap

DESIGNERS: by KlipKlap / Pia Lauritsen (Denmark)
YEAR OF DEVELOPMENT: 2011
MAIN MATERIALS: eco-tex certified cold foam, polyester

PHOTOS: J&W PHOTOGRAPHY

Crisis Junior Bed and Child's Chair

In designing the Crisis series, Piet Hein Eek set himself the challenge of using cheap materials to produce a good design. The material used is plywood underlayment. The Crisis Junior Bed and the Crisis Child's Chair are available in an unlacquered version as well as in four colors: white, pink, blue/grey, and green/grey. The techniques used for the pieces are meant to bring attention to the material at hand.

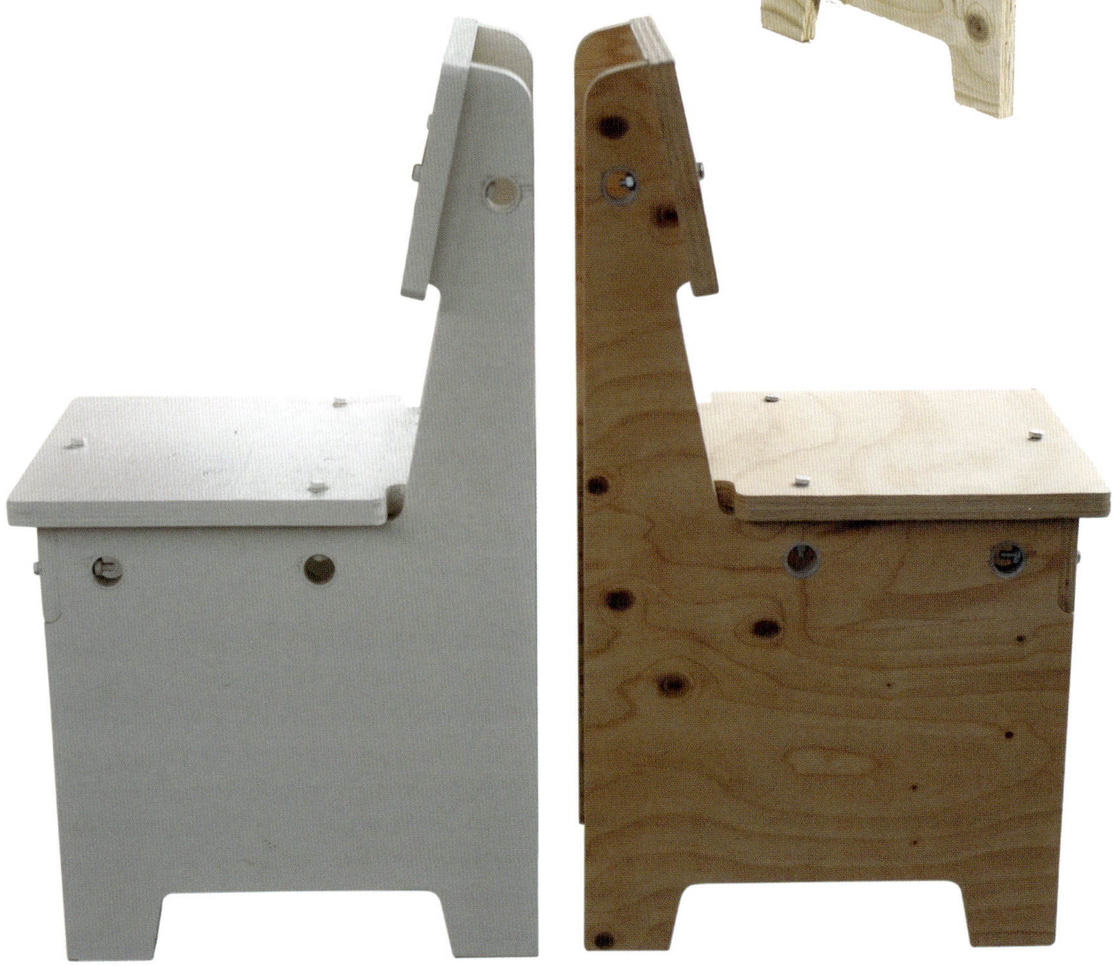

DESIGNERS: Piet Hein Eek (The Netherlands)
YEAR OF DEVELOPMENT: 2009 (Child's Chair)
MAIN MATERIALS: scrap wood (Child's Chair), plywood (Junior Bed)

PHOTOS: COURTESY OF THE DESIGNERS

Tomtom Chair, Little Angel Stool

The Tomtom Chair can be interpreted by kids in may different ways. Its one hundred different color combinations make this product unique. The clear design and pure colors of Little Angel Stool match any drawing table. The bright sky-blue base holds into place a white, cartoon-like structure in which the child can comfortably lean in and has two small angel wings on its back. The simple design and subtle colors of both pieces are a nice addition to any contemporary home.

Design:
Furf Design Studio

DESIGNERS: Furf Design Studio (Brazil)
YEAR OF DEVELOPMENT: 2011 (Little Angel Stool), 2012 (Tomtom Chair)
MAIN MATERIALS: wood

PHOTOS: COURTESY OF THE DESIGNERS

Bienvenida Crib

The solid simplicity and subtle sophistication of the Bienvenida Crib is surely hard to beat. Built in natural Patagonian wood, this children's bed can be enjoyed by child and parents alike - comfort and functionality are in perfect harmony with beautiful style. The crib includes a small and a big sleeping basket and two storage baskets, which can be arranged according to the child's age and needs.

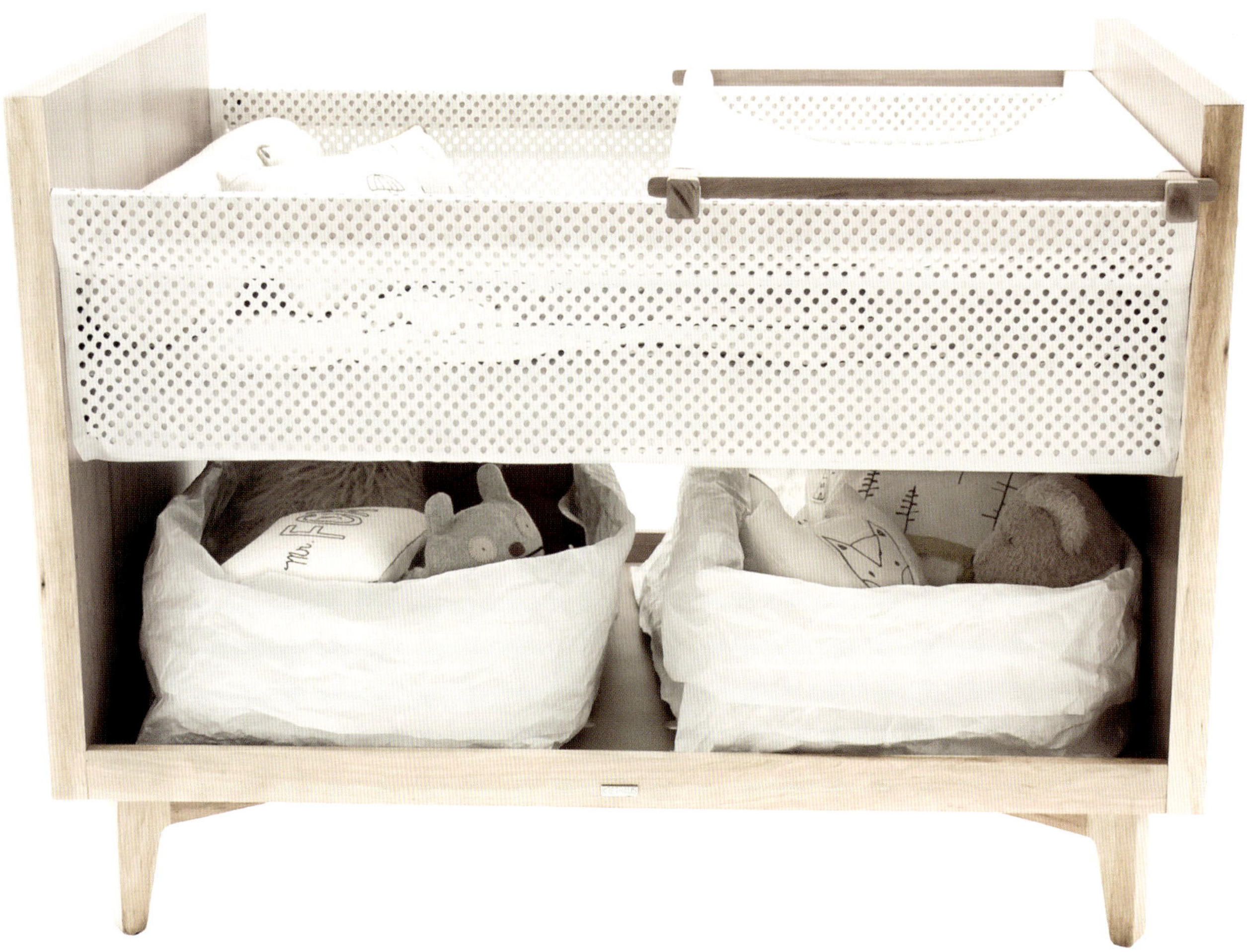

DESIGNERS: Krethaus (Argentina)
YEAR OF DEVELOPMENT: 2013
MAIN MATERIALS: Patagonian wood

Design: Krethaus

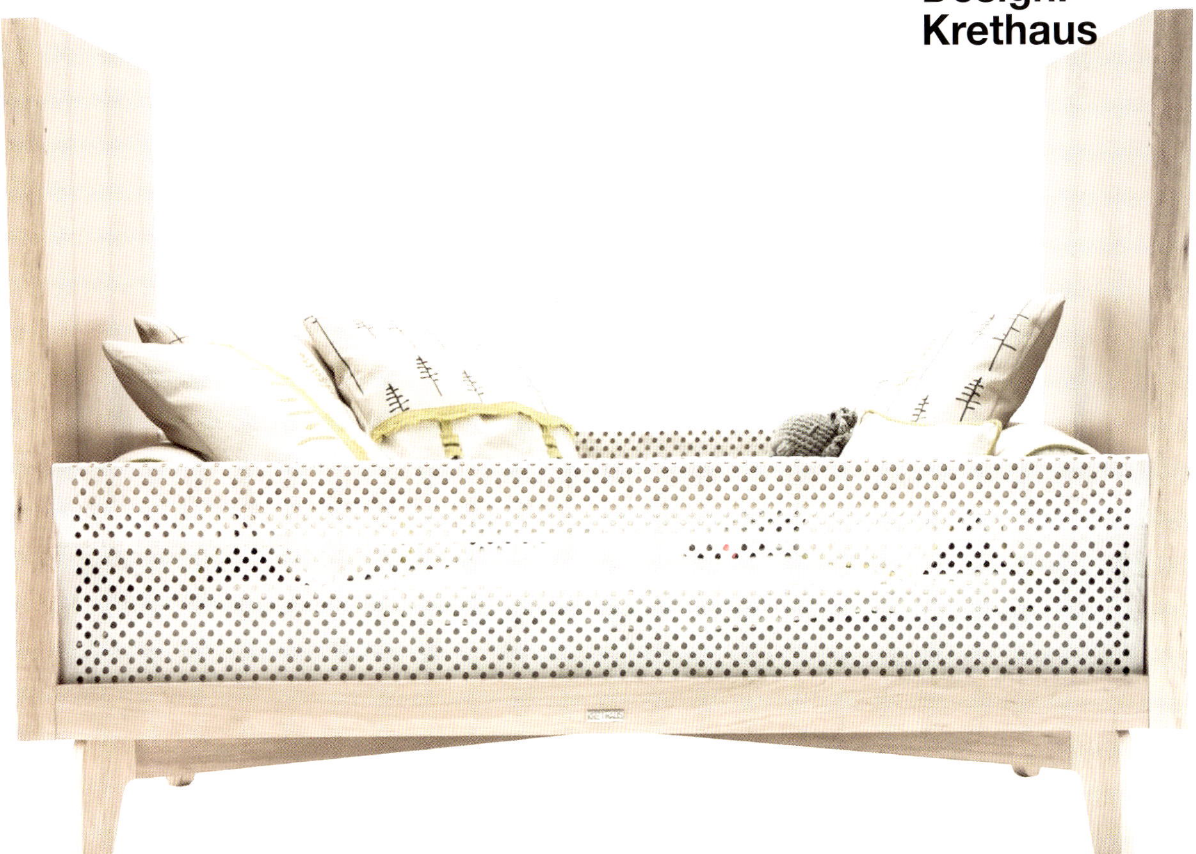

PHOTOS: VICTORIA EGURZA

Laurette Déco

Laurette is a playful collection of vintage-inspired furniture for children designed by Laure Bailleux. It is colorful and imaginative, definitely creative enough to stimulate and inspire children. Bailleux channels a retro vibe in her quirky collection. Desks and chairs take their style cues from 1950s classroom furniture, while pieces such as La Bibliothèque La Folie - a ladder-inspired bookcase - would look right at home in a 1950s living room. The furniture is available in an eclectic range of shades, from mouse grey and mole to bubblegum and old rose.

DESIGNERS: Laurette / Laure Bailleux (France)
MAIN MATERIALS: beech and MDF wood, metal & cotton cover (La chaise Papillon)

Design: Laurette

PHOTOS: COURTESY OF THE DESIGNERS

Children's Highchair, Child Child Chair

Winner of the international Red Dot Award in product design, this innovative highchair by Maartje Steenkamp is a triumph of simplicity and ingenuity. Part adaptable furniture that changes as your child grows and part conceptual art piece, it truly is one of a kind. As the child grows, the chair's legs are sawn down, encouraging the child to stand on his or her own two feet.

The phases of life are marked in the gradually changing shape of the product, a powerful visual reminder of time passing. The Child Child Chair is a combination of two children's chairs and a table. The children may sit, play and have a nice child-to-child conversation on their own level.

DESIGNERS: Studio Maartje Steenkamp (The Netherlands)
PRODUCERS: Droog Design
YEAR OF DEVELOPMENT: 2006
MAIN MATERIALS: birch multiplex wood

Design:
Studio Maartje Steenkamp

PHOTOS: INGA POWILLEIT

Perch Bunk Bed

The elegant Perch Bunk Bed is the perfect centerpiece for any child's room. Its compact footprint leaves plenty of room for play and additional furnishings. The versatile Perch easily separates into a loft bed and a standalone twin, giving many combination options. It comes in birch or walnut and co-ordinates perfectly with other beautiful pieces in the oeuf collection. Both beds are slightly lower than most bunks on the market, which makes them less daunting for bunk novices as well as easier to reach.

DESIGNERS: oeuf (USA)
MAIN MATERIALS: Baltic birch plywood and FSC certified eco-MDF

PHOTOS: COURTESY OF THE DESIGNERS

Sparrow

The Sparrow collection by oeuf creates a sophisticated nursery for your baby with a simple, clean design applied to the necessities of modern day parenting. Slim side rails and spindles give the crib a light, airy feel and make it a favorite of interior designers. Its high quality and sturdy construction means it will last for generations.

DESIGNERS: oeuf (USA)
MAIN MATERIALS: solid birch, Baltic birch plywood (legs)

PHOTOS: COURTESY OF THE DESIGNERS

Dog Lamp, Frank

Quirky, well-made and highly amusing - pana objects might just be onto something with their latest lamp... For kids who love dogs, Frank is simply the perfect present. Watch their eyes light up as they see the four movable legs and are entranced by the endearing design. Never has a lamp had so much character. Modern, functional and playful, Frank will light up any nursery.

DESIGNERS: pana objects (Thailand)
MAIN MATERIALS: beech wood

Design: pana objects

PHOTOS: COURTESY OF THE DESIGNERS

Scrap Wood Child Chairs

Piet Hein Eek is a Dutch designer best known for his scrap wood furniture series that he creates using scraps of reclaimed wood. Each piece of beautiful, timeless and unique furniture is lovingly handcrafted by Eek and is designed and made to last. Each scrap wood piece is one-of-a-kind and has a different color scheme and style. Piet Hein Eek uses waste materials such as wood from old furniture, doors, and industrial packaging to create wonderful and ecological furniture.

DESIGNERS: Piet Hein Eek (The Netherlands)
MAIN MATERIALS: scrap wood

PHOTOS: COURTESY OF THE DESIGNERS

Nido Table + Chair

With its simple, modern design, the Nido Table + Chair from Krethaus are the ideal addition to any contemporary family home. Quick and easy to erect in any room of the house, it represents the perfect space for kids to share creative time with the rest of the family. Your child can store their colors and pencils in a central case and personalize the flag to proudly mark their territory. Made from solid, natural Patagonian wood, this sturdy and attractive table and chair will delight children and parents alike.

DESIGNERS: Krethaus (Argentina)
YEAR OF DEVELOPMENT: 2010
MAIN MATERIALS: Patagonian wood

**Design:
Krethaus**

PHOTOS: VICTORIA EGURZA

OSKARatWORK

A beautiful set which includes a table and one bench for your child to spend long hours drawing or doing his or her homework. OSKARatWORK is made of plywood combined with a flexible yet highly durable loden (100% wool) fabric covering, a characteristic of perluding's designs. The set comes in a flat pack and is easily assembled or taken apart. A practical storage shelf in A4 size is located underneath the tabletop and bench seat.

Design: perludi

DESIGNERS: perludi / Thomas Maitz (Austria)
MAIN MATERIALS: birch plywood, loden (100% wool)

PHOTOS: MARTIN PABIS

Caspar

Austrian furniture designers perludi have introduced the Caspar children's table, which is designed to be able to grow in height as your child gets older. Pursuing the philosophy of ergonomic, versatile and environment-friendly children's furniture, perludi has produced a winner: Colorful legs that are simply placed into the four holes in the handcrafted solid-wood tabletop and secured at the desired height with o-rings made from natural rubber. To adjust the top's height and inclination, or to balance out an uneven floor, simply slide the infinitely adjustable legs up or down individually within their holes.

DESIGNERS: perludi / Martin Pabis and Thomas Maitz (Austria)
MAIN MATERIALS: solid wood, spruce

PHOTOS: MARTIN PABIS

Design: perludi

F & R Bed – Set for 2 Kids

This children's bed is far more than a place to sleep. The modern stylish bunk is designed to encourage creative play. It is the ideal centerpiece for your children's room. The lower bunk can be easily moved through wheels, allowing to make space to play under the bunk during the day. Choose from natural birch, white wash and dark chocolate - something for every decor and taste.

DESIGNERS: RaFa-kids / Agata & Arek Seredyn (The Netherlands)
MAIN MATERIALS: birch plywood

Design: RaFa-kids

PHOTOS: COURTESY OF THE DESIGNERS

Bedtimestories

One of the biggest perks of being a parent is that you get to be a kid all over again while raising your own. Bedtimestories is a cool, interactive storytelling backdrop that doubles as a child's bed. A cutout section can serve as an impromptu puppet stage, while the blanket can become a tent, magic carpet, patch of grass or whatever you need.

DESIGNERS: Ridder & Clown (The Netherlands)
MAIN MATERIALS: yellow poplar wood

Design:
Ridder & Clown

PHOTOS: COURTESY OF THE DESIGNERS

MAXintheBOX

The two modular furniture elements, combined called MAXintheBOX, were developed together with children and offer great possibilities for experimenting with and in space. Whether as a classic table-chair combination, as stools for adults, as a grocery store or a shelf for books - MAXintheBOX's possible applications are as endless as children's fantasies. It stimulates their imagination and shapes their identity. It is built with organic plywood and comprising a growing seat height, MAXintheBOX comes as an indestructible companion for your children for many years.

Design: perludi

DESIGNERS: perludi / Thomas Maitz (Austria)
MAIN MATERIALS: birch plywood

PHOTOS: MARTIN PA[illegible]S

Saccotto

DESIGNERS: Il Saccotto (Italy)
YEAR OF DEVELOPMENT: 2012
MAIN MATERIALS: velvet soft high strength synthetic, cotton

Saccotto is the idea of the architect couple Anna and Albert, who after the birth of their child have decided to approach the world of design for children. Saccotto, made in Italy, is halfway between a chair and a nice stuffed animal. The simplicity of the shapes, clean lines of its profile and the careful choice of fabrics and colors show that Saccotto can join as a piece of furniture into a classic children's room as well as the more urban loft, meeting the demands of children and adults who love design.

Design:
Il Saccotto

PHOTOS: COURTESY OF THE DESIGNERS

Wooden Animals

Kay Bojesen's wooden animal family is undeniably a design classic of our time. The figures are placed on the crossroad between imaginary figures and design objects while they unite form and function, seriousness and play. In 2011, three old friends joined the family when the Dachshund, the Hippo and the Rabbit were put into production again. All animals have a clean, contemporary expression without any superfluous shapes. Not only in children's rooms, but also in shelves and offices, the wooden animals are meanwhile desired collectors items that are passed from one generation to another.

DESIGNERS: Kay Bojesen (Denmark)
PRODUCERS: Rosendahl Design Group
YEAR OF DEVELOPMENT: 1934 (Dachshund; reproduction: 2011), 1951 (Monkey), 1952 (Bear), 1953 (Elephant)
MAIN MATERIALS: oak and maple wood (Bear), walnut wood (Dachshund), oak (Elephant), teak and limba wood (Monkey)

PHOTOS: COURTESY OF THE DESIGNERS

STEK Table and Bench

STEK is children's furniture that also appeals to grown-ups. The initiative of the Netherlands based architectural design studio, Ateliers Hessing & Brunings, is focused on creating a children's furniture collection in a basic design that fits in any interior.

The simple forms are chosen to invite children to sit and play. The affordable and handmade quality will last a lifetime or more. In 2013 all chairs were improved with a storage space behind the back rest.

Design: About STEK

DESIGNERS: About STEK (The Netherlands)
YEAR OF DEVELOPMENT: 2010, 2013
MAIN MATERIALS: birch wood

PHOTOS: MONI VAN BRUGGEN (80 A.L., 81), BARBARA VERBIJ (80 A.R., 80 B.)

The Tea Table, The Milk Stool

Studio delle Alpi, founded by Anne Kieffer, a product designer and Arnaud Mouriamé, a graphic designer, mixes low-budget materials with high-end techniques by adding manual silkscreen printing to plywood to intensify its character. The result is strikingly simple, colorful cutouts and geometric shapes with character. The studio manufactures in small quantities and collaborates with local artisans to make the highest quality pieces.

Design:
Studio delle Alpi

DESIGNERS: Studio delle Alpi / Anne Kieffer and Arnaud Mouriamé (Luxembourg)
YEAR OF DEVELOPMENT: 2013
MAIN MATERIALS: plywood

PHOTOS: ARNAUD MOURIAMÉ - STUDIO DELLE ALPI

Twogetherfelto, Twogetherpara

Twogetherfelto and Twogetherpara are based on the idea of a simple armchair with one extra wide arm support that a mother can lay her baby on. Steenkamp chose to explore how she could use cutting edge materials to integrate the structure of the chair with the softness needed to make it comfortable. Parabeam, a three-dimensional glass textile gave the structural function and Felto is the upholstery fabric used. The chair can be produced in a left and a right version and has evolved into a multi-purpose lounge or family chair.

DESIGNERS: Studio Maartje Steenkamp (The Netherlands)
MAIN MATERIALS: parabeam 3D glass textile, Felto (upholstery fabric)

Design:
Studio Maartje Steenkamp

PHOTOS: INGA POWILLEIT

Chestnut Paper Lamp

Nellianna and Kenneth, the two designers behind Studio Snowpuppe experimented with paper diamond shapes and developed the origami paper lampshades. They wanted to filter the light through paper to make a cozy and nice atmosphere to live in, especially in the light-deprived winter months in Middle and Northern Europe. This was the starting point for the Chestnut Paper Lamp. Inspired by chestnuts it has a cornered outside and a curved inside that you would not expect when looking at its outside. Studio Snowpuppe compares it to the first time you open a chestnut and see that it is very round and curved on the inside.

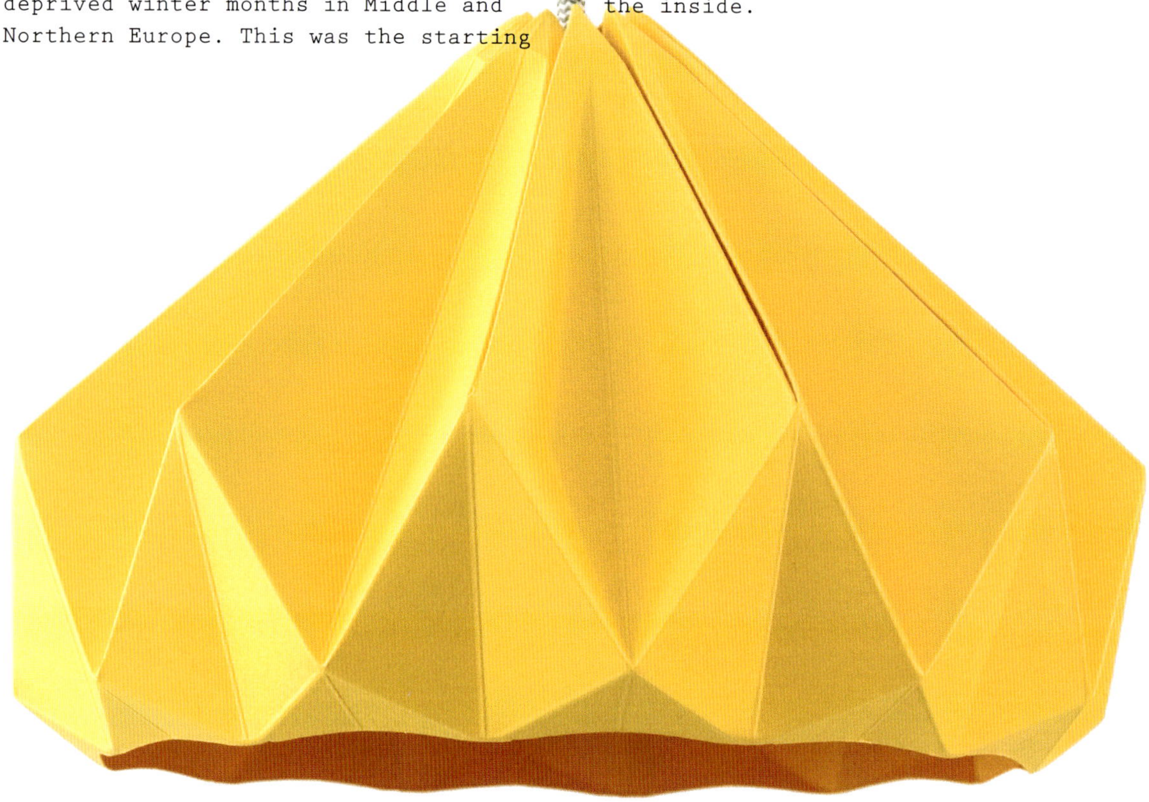

Design:
Studio Snowpuppe

DESIGNERS: Studio Snowpuppe / Nellianna van den Baard and Kenneth Veenenbos (The Netherlands)
YEAR OF DEVELOPMENT: 2011
MAIN MATERIALS: paper

PHOTOS: COURTESY OF THE DESIGNERS

Volley Rocker

Volley Rocker, designed by Adam Goodrum for Tait in Thornbury, Australia, has been designed and built to hold up to all possible Australian weather extremes. The beautiful clean lines and airy lightness of these rocking chairs are perfectly suited for a modern nursery room. They are available as a dining chair, lounger, bar stool or rocker and can be powder coated in a variety of UV stable colors. The beautifully streamlined design is well suited to use both indoors and outdoors. Its comfortable mesh seat panel, which is encapsulated by the zinc plated steel frame, is the perfect example of durability coupled with style and comfort.

DESIGNERS: Adam Goodrum (Australia)
PRODUCERS: Tait
YEAR OF DEVELOPMENT: 2012
MAIN MATERIALS: zinc plated steel fame, mesh seat panel, rope handles

Design:
Adam Goodrum

PHOTOS: COURTESY OF THE PRODUCERS

Come & Draw Table

The lovely table is not only an artistic drawing space, but also a special storage for your kids' precious artwork and memories. It features hundreds of unique round papers stacked on the tabletop. Fun, improvisational, playful, it speaks the same language as your kids. This little table easily fits in any home environment.

DESIGNERS: Tian Tang Design studio (Sweden)
YEAR OF DEVELOPMENT: 2011
MAIN MATERIALS: painted MDF, untreated pine, paper

**Design:
Tian Tang
Design studio**

PHOTOS: COURTESY OF THE DESIGNERS

The Puffin and the Songbirds

The Puffin and the Songbirds are the newest members of Kay Bojesen's wooden animals family. Both figures differ from most of the other family members in that the bodies are painted. The Puffin was designed originally in 1954 in collaboration with the scenographer Svend Johansen who was known for his naivistic style. The Songbird is a hitherto unknown design created in the 1960s but never put into production. The Songbirds are made of solid beech wood and hand-painted; all six birds, named after the designer and his family, have a clean, modern expression, stripped of superfluous details.

DESIGNERS: Kay Bojesen (Denmark)
PRODUCERS: Rosendahl Design Group
ORIGINAL DESIGN: 1954 (Puffin), 1950 (Songbirds)
PRODUCTION: 2013 (re-introduction Puffin), 2012 (first production Songbirds)
MAIN MATERIALS: solid beech wood

PHOTOS: COURTESY OF THE DESIGNERS

Geo's Table, Scoreboard, Lilly's Chair

Crafted from bamboo by WE:DO:WOOD, this boutique Danish design firm holds true to their vision that good design should be sustainable and respectful of the environment. The company has a staunch motto to "do no harm" to the animal or plant life where its bamboo is grown, so pesticides and other toxins are banned.

The minimalistic desk, designed by Henry Thygesen and Sebastian Jørgensen has a useful pullout drawer to stow paper, crayons and other drawing paraphernalia. The set of a desk and two chairs comes in a choice of black, red or blue trims.

DESIGNERS: WE:DO:WOOD / Henry Thygesen and Sebastian Jørgensen (Denmark)
MAIN MATERIALS: bamboo

PHOTOS: COURTESY OF THE DESIGNERS

Fashion

Children's fashion is a rather recent phenomenon. It used to be that children would have a set of clothes for playtime and a set for sleep time, and the most important thing was that they were functional. Today, kids fashion is one of the most innovative sectors in fashion design. It is a pioneer for many technical and ethical developments and improvements. High standards in quality and in the social sector must be attained. Kids fashion should be free of chemical dyes, produced in a fair trade environment, and only the best materials should be used to produce it. Achievement of these high standards together with a contemporary design that also appeals to children is a great challenge for the designers.

Nowadays, fashion is all around us and children are inevitably influenced by it. Especially little girls become aware of it from a very early age on. They want to choose their own wardrobe according to what they deem fashionable and cool. Boys, who used to be especially lim-

ited in their choice of clothes, can now enjoy unique fashion by kid's designers too. Bright colors, cool prints and comfortable materials are the main ingredients to design great children's clothes.

Tutu Du Monde is a line of tutus, with which little children can imagine being a dainty ballerina, a magical fairy and a benevolent princess; the designs are not only timeless and exquisitely made but are also ecologically sustainable and created with love. When purchasing a knitted item from *Mormor.nu* you not only get an exquisite piece of clothing, you get a fairy-grandmother too. The pieces are kept in simple, nordic designs, and are hand-knitted by 50 grandmothers. If you are looking for a retro touch in your child's wardrobe, you will be happy to learn that Graziela Preiser has re-launched her famous brand *byGraziela* together with her daughter. You can find all the familiar designs from your childhood memories and pass them on to your children.

Kallio Collection

Kallio is a New York kids' clothing brand making a difference. Founded by Karina Kallio, the brand takes up-cycling to a whole new level! Men's vintage shirts are turned into a whole range of trendy kids' clothing. A pair of cool harem pants for boys are tailored out of an old pair of sleeves. An oversized flannel shirt is transformed into a poncho for girls. This really is sustainable fashion at its best!

DESIGNERS: Kallio / Karina Kallio (USA)
YEAR OF DEVELOPMENT: 2013
MAIN MATERIALS: reclaimed vintage materials

PHOTOS: DAN MCMAHON

Bicycle Saddle Bag

For all children who want to collect treasures while riding their bike, Meisen auf Reisen has designed the Bicycle Saddle Bag. Three straps on the back of the bag can be attached with Velcro to the handlebars and steering tube. The bag is available in different color combinations (cover covered with fabric) and prints, a good shot of retro, a pinch of nostalgia and a dash of GDR.

DESIGNERS: Meisen auf Reisen / Sina Lähme (Germany)
YEAR OF DEVELOPMENT: 2011
MAIN MATERIALS: synthetic leather, bias tape, screen printing ink

Design:
Meisen auf Reisen

PHOTOS: SINA LÄHME, JULIA WECK (PORTRAIT)

Petit Clothes

"Once upon a time there was a friendly clothing brand that spoke the language that children speak". That's the reason behind their talent to create characters that children soon make their heroes. Playful yet always elegant, these designs reveal their strong Spanish identity. The materials are always soft, comfortable and natural. BOBO CHOSES also supports ethical causes. They founded actbybobo.org in order to financially assist various projects such as, a women's school in the north of Bangladesh and Aytimoun Yo.

Design: BOBO CHOSES

DESIGNERS: BOBO CHOSES / Laia Aguilar & Adriana Eperalba (Spain)
YEAR OF DEVELOPMENT: 2013
MAIN MATERIALS: 100% cotton

PHOTOS: COURTESY OF THE DESIGNERS

1,2,3 Hooded Towel

In 1970 Graziela Preiser's designs conquered the hearts of young and old. Her fabrics, bedding and crockery all in typical bold and colorful designs were present in almost all German homes, embodying the childhood memories of a generation. The cult designs are finally available again: Co-founded byGraziela and her daughter Nina, the byGraziela label relaunches the iconic and award winning patterns on a range of products. The vibrant colors and unique designs will appeal to parents looking to create an authentic retro feel in nurseries and kids rooms.

DESIGNERS: byGraziela (Germany)
YEAR OF DEVELOPMENT: 1972
MAIN MATERIALS: 100% cotton

Design: byGraziela

PHOTOS: COURTESY OF THE DESIGNERS

EGG Helmets

These cool and retro helmets for kids between the ages of 2 and 12 can be endlessly personalized through skins, printed stretch fabric helmet covers and soft rubber snap-on accessories. Easily customize your very own helmet: Choose your helmet, choose your skin, choose your add-on. The helmets are designed, engineered and made in the Netherlands; the skins are made of high-quality stretch fabric and are washable, the add-ons are made of premium soft rubber and simply snap on to the helmet's outer shell. They do not compromise the helmet's effectiveness as they are designed to pop off in the event of an impact.

DESIGNERS: EGG (The Netherlands)
YEAR OF DEVELOPMENT: 2010
MAIN MATERIALS: shell: ABS outer shell, a flexible EPP safety core, and an EVA comfort core; skins: printed elastane fabric; helmet covers add-ons: soft rubber snap-on accessories

Design:
EGG

PHOTOS: COURTESY OF THE DESIGNERS

Mormor.nu

Mormor.nu (in Danish mormor means grandmother on the mother's side) started as a team of local Danish knitting grannies - some of whom have been knitting all their lives. The use of old knitting techniques, with vintage designs adapted to contemporary taste - and great attention to detail is what makes these clothes unique. All pieces are knitted by hand, mostly in the softest alpaca wool. Mormor.nu has gathered more than 50 grandmothers who produce hand knitted baby and children's clothes from newborn up to five years. When buying an item from Mormor.nu you will always receive a personal note from the grandmother who has knitted your newly purchased item.

Design: Mormor.nu

DESIGNERS: Mormor.nu / Nina Brandi (Denmark)
YEAR OF DEVELOPMENT: 2003
MAIN MATERIALS: pure new wool, merino wool

PHOTOS: COURTESY OF THE DESIGNERS

Aprés Swim Collection

A deep affinity for everything beachy, a constantly sunburned nose and a failure to find innovative and fun sun protective products for her own kids led Sara Bellamy to create starhorn&bell in 2009 - a world where the small folk in your life can play safely in the sun for hours! All of her products come in beautiful fabrics designed by Sara and printed in Switzerland to the highest standards. All pieces carry certified UPF levels and a percentage of the takings from each item sold is donated to skin cancer research.

DESIGNERS: starhorn&bell / Sara Bellamy (Switzerland)
YEAR OF DEVELOPMENT: 2013

Design: starhorn&bell

PHOTOS: COURTESY OF THE DESIGNERS

Keep it Surreal

This new, whimsical collection by oeuf is a mix of funny and spooky themes. Keep it Surreal includes many pullovers, tunic dresses, leggings, hoodies and accessories in classic neutral colors, perfect to mix and match endlessly. Gloves with open eyes, sweaters with glasses and moustaches, hoodies with bunny ears, attachable tails, and a bunch of playful accessories complete a stylish Halloween look that no one would mind wearing through the rest of fall and winter. The knits are handcrafted by Bolivian artisans using 100% super-soft and hypoallergenic baby alpaca wool.

DESIGNERS: oeuf (USA)
MAIN MATERIALS: 100% baby alpaca wool

PHOTOS: COURTESY OF THE DESIGNERS

In the Wings

The magical world of Tutu Du Monde, where little girls can dress up and lose themselves in another time and place is the creation of fashion designer Andrea Rembeck. The line of vintage-inspired tutus which are timeless, wearable, ethically made, ecologically sustainable and exquisitely crafted with love and passion. Like a discovery from an old chest in the backstage wardrobe department, Tutu Du Monde creations only get better with age and wear, with slight fading and fraying edges adding to their charm. The range now includes tutu skirts and dresses, embellished cotton tops and playsuits, cardigans and caplets, and accessories.

Design: Andrea Rembeck

DESIGNERS: Tutu Du Monde / Andrea Rembeck
YEAR OF DEVELOPMENT: 2013
MAIN MATERIALS: soft cotton, fine tulle, pure silk, and hand-sewn embellishments

PHOTOS: ALEXANDRENA PARKER

Play

Play is an essential part of children's education. It enables them to find out about themselves and the world. While playing children may discover, experiment and invent. In this process, a child's cognitive and motor skills are developed and enhanced. At the same time they learn social interaction when playing in a group.

The ideal toy unites all these qualities and keeps creativity at the forefront of your child's mind. In addition, it meets the highest demands of durability, safety, and sustainability. Besides all those practical criteria, a toy must have a certain aesthetic appeal that instantly attract parents and children alike. The heart of each toy is simple ingenuity, which leaves enough space for each child's individual imagination. It is the designers' challenge to create a great design from this simplicity.

Traditional toys like train sets, animal replicas, dolls and dollhouses are found throughout all cultures and eras because they mirror everyday life. The designs featured in this section are contemporary as well as classic. They all share

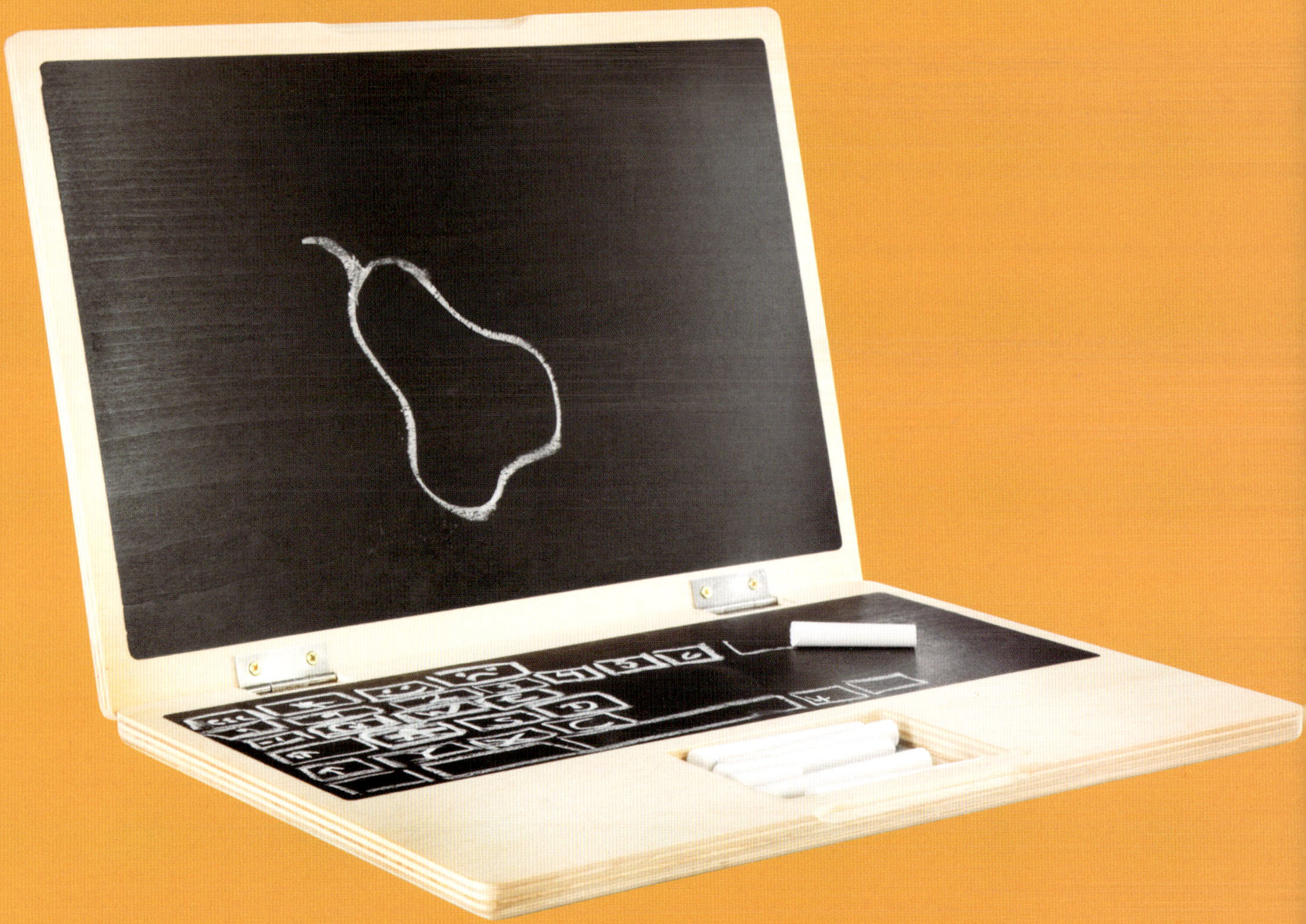

the ability to open up a child's fantasy world. The range of products extends from dolls to role play items to construction toys. The *Fair Trade Wooden Dolls* by Goose Grease, are deliberately held in a very simple and pure design, which sets no boundaries to children's creativity as they design their own unique pieces. Every child's dream of a fabulous hideaway was made real by Bach Architects. The *Playhouse* for small-scale people is the ideal place to play, imagine and create. The small wooden cottage seems right out of a fairy tale. Its timeless design will surely delight the lucky kids who have them for many years to come! If you have a young do-it-yourselfer at home the *cuboro* marble track will surely get his or her attention. The simple beech wood cubes can be reassembled time and again and leave endless room for experimentation and exploration.

These are innovative toy designs that parents as well as children will appreciate.

Playhouse

When Anna and Eugeni Bach's children asked for a playhouse, they surely didn't expect this beauty! Made of spruce wood sourced from trees planted by the children's great-grandfather and built on the perfect site on their grandparents' farm, this fabulous hideaway is every child's dream. The small-scale interior - designed for small-scale people - is the ideal place to play, imagine and create. The small wooden cottage seems to come right out of a fairy tale - its timeless simplicity will surely delight those lucky kids for many years to come.

DESIGNERS: Bach Architects /
Anna & Eugeni Bach (Spain)
YEAR OF DEVELOPMENT: 2011
MAIN MATERIALS: milled spruce wood

Design: Bach Architects

PHOTOS: TIIA ETTALA

Bilibo

Bilibo is a multifunctional play object that turns into anything a child wants it to be. It does not require instructions or batteries. Highly acclaimed by childhood learning specialists, the iconic shell is on its way to becoming a new classic, leading a trend back to more simple, sustainable toys.

The soft curvature of the shell enables safe use as a seat for rocking and spinning, tortoise shell, hideaway and much more. The elementary shapes and bright colors appeal to the curiosity and play instinct of children. Bilibo promotes motor activity in various movement games or can be used as a versatile prop for role play. Depending on the specific interest and age of the child, different qualities become more prominent. This way, Bilibo is a companion for children for many years, practically growing along with them - whether indoors or outdoors, in the sand pit, near water, or in the snow.

Design: Alex Hochstrasser

DESIGNERS: Alex Hochstrasser (Switzerland)
YEAR OF DEVELOPMENT: 2001 (Bilibo), 2006 (Bilibo Mini)
MAIN MATERIALS: high-density polyethylene

PHOTOS: ALEX HOCHSTRASSER (120 B.) / ACTIVE PEOPLE (120 A., 121)

bObles

bObles began in 2006, when Bolette Blædel, an architect, went on maternity leave with her first-born son and realized that children's furniture was inadequate as it is mostly merely miniatures of adult furniture. Her sister, a designer by profession, and Bolette began to imagine: What if they could create children's furniture that would indulge children's imagination through playing and learning while developing children's motor skills? The idea manifested into bObles, tumbling furniture based on simple geometric forms cut into the shape of animals. Children can tumble, roll, balance, seesaw, rock, jump and gain bodily experience, which can serve as the foundation for further motor development.

DESIGNERS: bObles (Denmark)
YEAR OF DEVELOPMENT: 2006
MAIN MATERIALS: environmentally-friendly firm foam, wood

PHOTOS: COURTESY OF THE DESIGNERS

House of Games

The beautifully crafted house of games by Dombon-a-tanya makes a charming feature in any modern home. Kids will love the surprising treasure trove of games hidden inside the house, while parents will be delighted by the sophisticated design and perfect functionality of the storage system. The House of Games harks back to a golden age of child's play with games made of wood and paper - dominoes, mikado, cards, board games - you'll be itching to join in the fun.

DESIGNERS: Dombon-a-tanya / Anikó Juhász and Anna Nóra Nagy (Hungary)
WOOD WORKS: Mihály Szabó
YEAR OF DEVELOPMENT: 2011
MAIN MATERIALS: wood, paper

Design: Dombon-a-tanya

PHOTOS: COURTESY OF THE DESIGNERS

The Rocket, Casa Cabana

A playhouse with a twist - kidsonroof have created a fantastic playhouse made entirely from cardboard. Casa Cabana comes either completely white or with a cat on a tree, a small ant, a rabbit and a squirrel. In any case more than enough room to color, paint and decorate it yourself. Let it be your tree house, mansion or hiding shed. Casa Cabana has a door, seven windows and many spy holes. Kidsroof created the Rocket with their approach to the act of playing, stimulating creativity and imagination, as the first training module for all future astronauts. Rocket is the perfect cardboard dream-machine.

DESIGNERS: kidsonroof
MAIN MATERIALS: recycled cardboard

Design: kidsonroof

PHOTOS: COURTESY OF THE DESIGNERS

I-Wood / I-Woody

Here's a smartphone you won't hesitate handing to your child. If you love wooden minimalist toys, you'll love this clever marriage between timber and technology. Donkey Products has launched two beautifully crafted toys that mimic a smartphone and laptop, without prematurely exposing your child to technology. They look just like the real thing, but are crafted from wood.

The "screen" is chalkboard, which can be drawn on and wiped clean. The I-Woody Smartphone also comes with sponge earphones. The I-Wood Laptop encourages your child's imagination, and its compactness makes it a great companion for the road.

DESIGNERS: Donkey Products / Bea Seggering & Donkey Creative Lab (Germany)
YEAR OF DEVELOPMENT: 2009-2012
MAIN MATERIALS: wood, stainless steel

PHOTOS: COURTESY OF THE DESIGNERS

Fair Trade Wooden Dolls

Anna Leigh and Juan Carlos Donado, founders of Goose Grease, are artists based in Brooklyn, NY. Together with local carpenters in Bogotá, Colombia, they work without intermediaries and support the local artisan community by working within the cottage style industry. Each doll from the Goose Grease standard sets is designed with sobriety at the forefront, allowing the child to use their imagination to give life to the dolls.

Design:
Goose Grease

DESIGNERS: Goose Grease / Juan and Anna Leigh Donado (Colombia)
YEAR OF DEVELOPMENT: 2013
MAIN MATERIALS: Urapan wood

PHOTOS: COURTESY OF THE DESIGNERS, PORTRAIT: KRISTINA GIBB

Léa Ecolo Doll

Léa is an organic doll designed for younger children. Face, hands and legs of the doll are made of perfumed vinyl, which is very soft and pleasant for the child, while its body and clothes are made of organic cotton. The dolls are manufactured in Europe to avoid large quantities of CO_2 emissions. Clever: the recycled cardboard box turns into a doll's bed.

DESIGNERS: PETITCOLLIN (France)
PRODUCERS: Vilac
YEAR OF DEVELOPMENT: 2011
MAIN MATERIALS: organic cotton, phtalate-free, soft vinyl

PHOTOS: VILAC

Bumble, Bimble and Billionaire

Hoptimist is a Danish company that was founded by the furniture designer Hans Gustav Ehrenreich already in 1968. His vision was to design classic characters that never go out of fashion. Today, they have taken advantage of his creativity and design and developed the figures Bumble, Bimble and Billionaire. Hoptimist works by the philosophy "smiles that warm the heart - smiles that heal" as a basic concept when designing their different characters.

DESIGNERS: Hoptimist / Lotte Steffensen and Jørn Ehrenreich (Denmark)
YEAR OF DEVELOPMENT: 2009
MAIN MATERIALS: oak wood, plastic

Design: Hoptimist

PHOTOS: COURTESY OF THE DESIGNERS

Design: iwishiwasa...

Cool Costumes for Kids

The inspiration for iwishiwasa… was the four-year-old son of costume designer Tamsin Thorne, who was already an enthusiastic dresser-upper and accomplished stylist. With nothing more than a marigold glove, an old fur hat and a stick, she saw how his dressing-up games allowed him to enter his own reality full of adventure and imagination.

Thorne's mission was to create original, beautiful, vibrant and fun costumes which capture the imagination and allow children to "become the creators of their own world". The costumes are all handmade and produced in small runs in London.

PHOTOS: BARRY GEORGE WOODS (134, 135 B.L., PORTRAIT),
MKFOTO.CO.UK (135 A.L., A.R., B.R.)

DESIGNERS: iwishiwasa… / Tamsin Thorne
(United Kingdom)
YEAR OF DEVELOPMENT: 2010
MAIN MATERIALS: vibrant, hardwearing
fabrics - vinyl, lycra, cotton,
bonded fabrics

Big-Bobby-Car

With its child-friendly design, indestructible quality and versatility, the BIG-BOBBY-CAR-CLASSIC is one of the world's most frequently purchased ride-on cars. It features maximum grip, a steering wheel, four stable tires, a trailer coupling, and a knee recess for older children for maximum playing fun. The high quality of manufacture and the low center of gravity make the BIG-BOBBY-CAR an especially safe toy. The NEW-BIG-BOBBY-CAR with a modern car design retains and improves all essential characteristics of the classic BIG-BOBBY-CAR.

DESIGNERS: crosscreative designstudios (Germany)
ORIGINAL DESIGNER: Ernst A. Bettag
YEAR OF DEVELOPMENT: 2005 (current model), 1972 (original model)
MAIN MATERIALS: plastic

PHOTOS: BIG-SPIELWARENFABRIK GMBH & CO. KG

Dollhouse

Design: Eva Schildt

The curved and smooth form of the Dollhouse is reminiscent of several ancienct structures, such as mud houses in Africa or igloos in Greenland. Inspired in that way, the Dollhouse was given this "original" human form. Consisting of two floors, it has a height of 30 centimeters and is manufactured out of solid wood and MDF boards. The white model house, which has three windows and a chimney on top of the round roof, can be used by both children to play with and adults to display it.

DESIGNERS: Eva Schildt (Sweden)
YEAR OF DEVELOPMENT: 2008 (current model), 2007 (original model)
MAIN MATERIALS: wood

PHOTOS: CCURTESY OF PLAYSAM

flix

The designers of SIRCH favored a design concept based on powerful aesthetic principles - the kind of toys that would look good in any house - beautiful enough to leave out, not tidy away. The children's ride-on, flix, from the Sibis toy collection, is one step in this conceptual direction. The rubber wheels are almost noiseless. Through their outer position they prevent damages to the furniture when it is accidentally hit.

Design: SIRCH

DESIGNERS: SIRCH / Christoph Blitzer, Wolfgang Sirch
YEAR OF DEVELOPMENT: 2000
MAIN MATERIALS: birch plywood

PHOTOS: MARKUS DLOUHY

Cocorico Cooker

An eco-friendly and delightful alternative to plastic kitchens, the Cocorico Cooker is a cardboard stove for the young cook. Lightweight and small, but still big enough to start cooking with mom or dad in the kitchen. Put it on the table, on the ground or anywhere where the little cook installs her or his cooking pots or saucepans. The design features an oven that opens, a printed stovetop, a clock and a rooster on the back.

DESIGNERS: kidsonroof / Elisabeth Vidal (The Netherlands)
MAIN MATERIALS: recycled cardboard

Design: kidsonroof

PHOTOS: COURTESY OF THE DESIGNERS

cuboro

The cuboro marble track system is made of beech wood cubes with 5 centimeters sides. The elements contain track functions on the surface and the inside and offer an unlimited number of combination possibilities. With the cuboro system everyone can build his or her own marble run. It consists of cubic elements featuring trenches and tunnels that can be assembled to create an infinite number of new marble runs. With the help of various level changing elements, the marble does not have to travel on a single level but can find its way at various heights through tunnels and trenches. Playing with the cuboro system not only develops skills and curiosity, but also the playful exploration of physical laws. After completion of the marble run, the builders are not only rewarded by the look of the new construction, but primarily by watching the travel of the marble, encouraging them to construct continuously new experiments.

DESIGNERS: Matthias Etter (Switzerland)
YEAR OF DEVELOPMENT: 1986 (current model), 1976 (prototype)
MAIN MATERIALS: beech wood

**Design:
Matthias Etter**

PHOTOS: COURTESY OF CUBORO AG

Mozartkugel

This sphere probably contains more Mozart than the chocolate of the same name. The withdrawable key is used to wind up the musical mechanism and the Mozart melody “Voi che sapete” from “The Marriage of Figaro” resounds from the heart of the 92-millimeter big wooden sphere. While the mechanism remains hidden forever inside the globe, the music transcends the limits of the geometrical shape. The beech or oak wood lends a harmonious resonance to the sound. This decoration and toy made of noble materials equally appeals to the sense of touch and the sense of hearing.

DESIGNERS: Adam + Harborth (Germany)
YEAR OF DEVELOPMENT: 2006
MAIN MATERIALS: beech wood / oak wood, metal

Design:
Adam + Harborth

PHOTOS: BERND GALLANDI

Mr. Cube

Mr. Cube is a collection of wooden figures with a common central body and interchangeable arms, legs and head. The parts can be rearranged and offer a number of combination possibilities thanks to the internal magnets. When the toy is not in use, all the parts can be taken apart and rearranged to form a cube shape, which makes this a great toy for travelling. The possiblities are endless and will encourage your child's imagination.

DESIGNERS: Héctor Serrano (United Kingdom)
YEAR OF DEVELOPMENT: 2011
MAIN MATERIALS: wood

Design: Héctor Serrano

PHOTOS: COURTESY OF THE DESIGNERS

MobileHome blue

kidsonroof's MobileHome blue is the perfect place to house your knights, pirates or princesses. The famous blue home is now also available in white with a red interior. Easy to carry and install, the home is parent-friendly too. With eight rooms, stair-openings, spy-holes and an attic for storage, the little ones in your life will never run out of games to play and stories to imagine. It's good for the environment too - made of 100% recycled cardboard, which is 100% biodegradable.

Design: kidsonroof

DESIGNERS: kidsonroof (The Netherlands)
MAIN MATERIALS: cardboard

PHOTOS: COURTESY OF THE DESIGNERS

Ping Pong Door

The Ping Pong Door fits into any standard door frame (86 x 198.5 centimeters) or is made to fit. When opened, the ping pong table turns 90 degrees and simultaneously drops to the playing level. The playing board made of HPL laminated wood is also available in colors other than the traditional green. The simple folding mechanism had to be specially developed to allow easy folding of the table with one move from the door leaf and to function as a solid table. The Ping Pong Door is also smaller than a regular table, which is more convenient for children. After playing the table can be simply folded back up and the door can be used in its regular function again.

Design: Tobias Fränzel

DESIGNERS: Tobias Fränzel Design GmbH / Tobias Fränzel (Germany)
YEAR OF DEVELOPMENT: 2005 (original model), 2009 (current model)
MAIN MATERIALS: wood, metal fitting with flap mechanism

PHOTOS: MARCEL KÖHLER

Rainbow

Nine curved maple plywood elements are play elements and resonating bodies. Bright rainbow colors and high quality wood turn Rainbow into a toy and art object with many sensory qualities. The simple shape combined with the bright, warm colors constitute the special appeal of this toy, which enchants younger and older children with constantly new variations. The modular concept provides various play options: whether the arches are used as building bricks, to establish a static balance, or as a winding rainbow track for the included ball is up to the imagination of the children. The simple geometric shape and combination possibilities of the individual parts also help to develop skills and imagination.

DESIGNERS: Heiko Hillig (Germany)
YEAR OF DEVELOPMENT: 1996
MAIN MATERIALS: maple plywood

Design:
Heiko Hillig

PHOTOS: COURTESY OF NAEF SPIELE AG, PORTRAIT: CHRISTOPH END

Rocking Horse Bobbel

The Rocking Horse Bobbel abstracts the concept of rocking horses so much that it seems to have derived from a sled. The two runners are gradually brought closer at the ends, bearing the seating area in the back, while in front they separate again into a steering that seems to have derived from bicycles. The foot area that connects the runners, instead of the traditional rocking horse foot rests, and the seat seem to have derived from furniture. This results in a very new, more comfortable type of rocking toy, which offers the same movements as a classical rocking horse yet is far removed from the typical shape of the animal.

DESIGNERS: Chris Slutter (The Netherlands)
YEAR OF DEVELOPMENT: 2004
MAIN MATERIALS: aluminum and teak

**Design:
Chris Slutter**

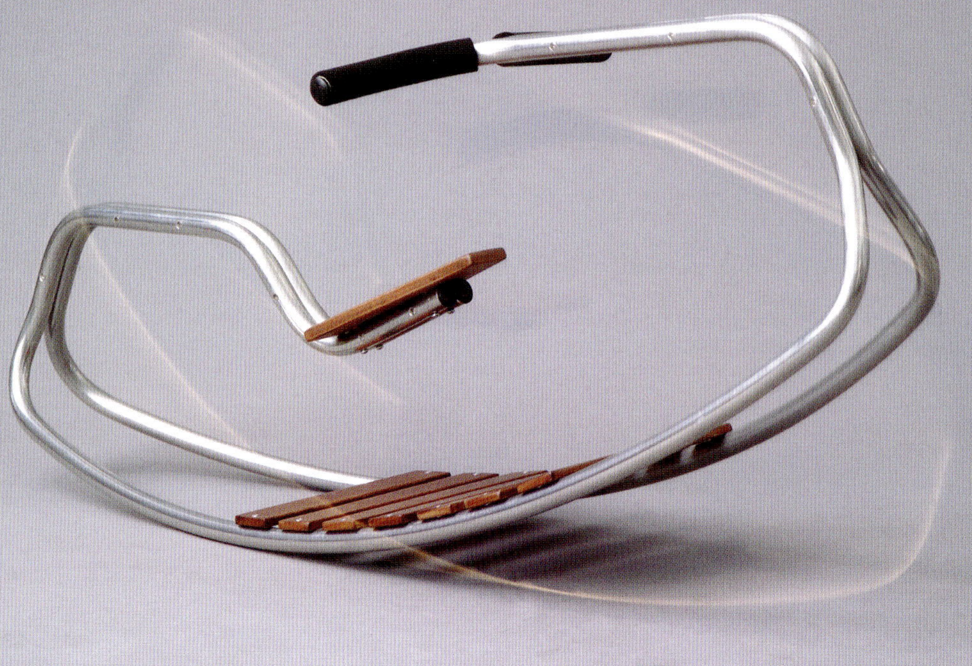

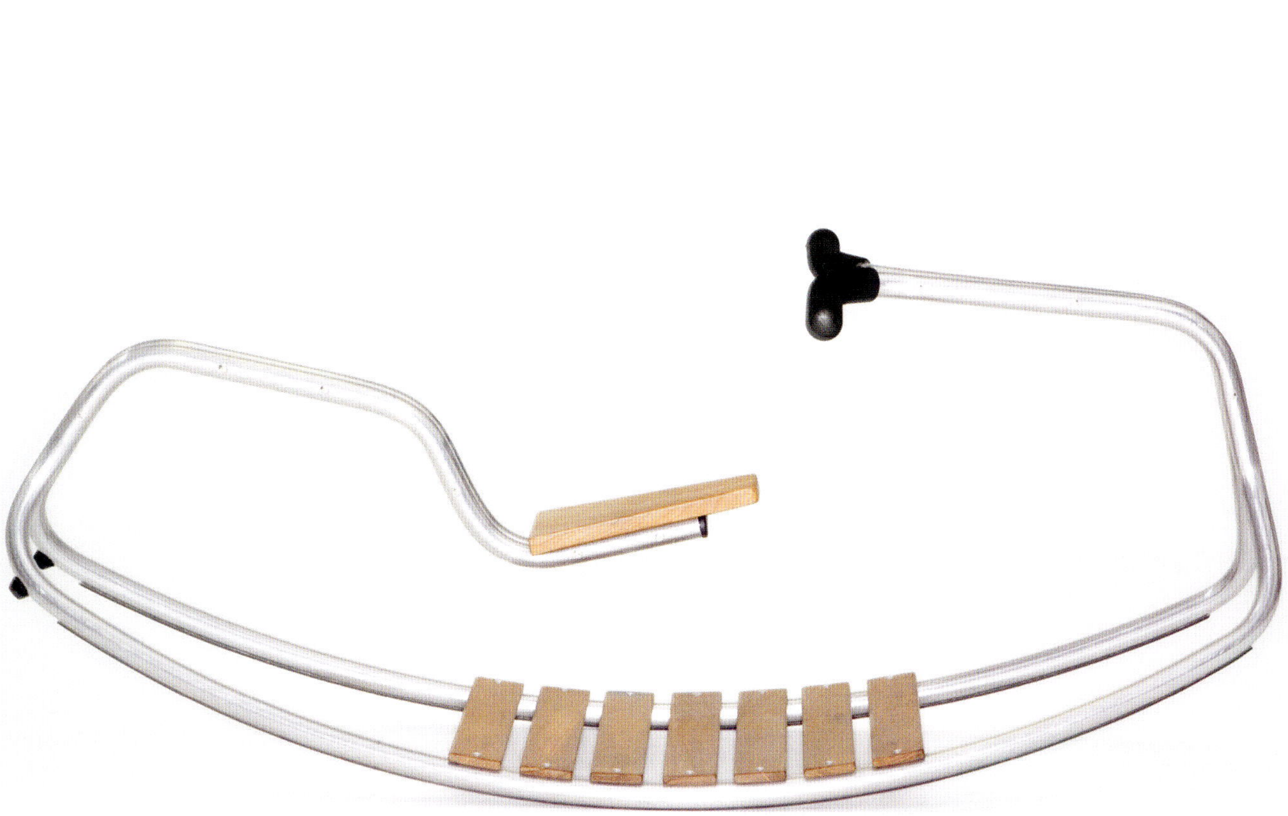

PHOTOS: COURTESY OF CHRIS SLUTTER ONTWERP

Machi & Kuruma

Machi is a minimalist children's toy designed by Japanese-based firm Kukkia. Kukkia means "to bloom" in Finnish and "kuki" means stem in Japanese. The focus of their products is to provide children with tactile and vividly colored shapes that are both fun and visually stimulating. Machi is a clear example of Kukkia's desire to motivate children to use their imagination. The set includes 15 beautifully designed pieces that can be arranged and re-arranged at will. Kids can create their own town by using the two magnetic chalkboards and the provided eco-chalk. The 15 wooden pieces, which are made of beech wood, include a car (Kuruma), six trees, two traffic signals, three buildings, and two mountains.

Design: Kukkia

DESIGNERS: Kukkia / Kaz Shiomi (Japan)
MAIN MATERIALS: beech wood

PHOTOS: COURTESY OF THE DESIGNERS

Schoolbag

This unique schoolbag by Dombon-a-tanya and TheBétaVersion will soon be loved by children everywhere. Made of pitted raw wood blocks and tanned leather straps, it's certainly unusual. Curious kids who adore collecting trinkets will love arranging them in the bag's different storage spaces. While the leather straps make it easy to carry, it is also a nice display object in your child's room.

**Design:
Dombon-a-tanya
and TheBétaVersion**

DESIGNERS: Dombon-a-tanya and TheBétaVersion (Hungary)
WOOD WORKS: Ferenc Bazsó, Zoltán Lang and Dániel Bortolits
YEAR OF DEVELOPMENT: 2011
MAIN MATERIALS: pitted raw wood blocks with tanned leather stripes

PHOTOS: COURTESY OF THE DESIGNERS

BU! The Blankie

Little Red Stuga adds three new motifs to Bu! The Blankie line created in collaboration with world renowned illustrators and artists. Teddy, Pirate and Lion join Indian in the new Bu! family. The traveling friend and comforting blankie doubles as a peekaboo sheet, and offers different levels of pedagogical and playful interaction depending on the child's age - peekaboo games for the smaller children, character and role-play for the toddlers. The blankets offer play and comfort all in one incredible design.

DESIGNERS: Little Red Stuga (Sweden)
DESIGN MOTIFS: Elisabeth Dunker (Indian and Lion), Will Broome (Pirate), Lisa Grue (Teddy)
YEAR OF DEVELOPMENT: 2011
MAIN MATERIALS: 100% cotton

Design:
Little Red Stuga

PHOTOS: ELISABETH DUNKER

Kattuska Boat and Castle

Kattuska had the vision to design and manufacture high quality toys, accessories and furniture for children, taking ergonomic and environmental aspects into account with their designs. The Boat is a swing with two seats, which can be used for two kids at the same time to experience water adventures. The Castle is a playhouse easily assembled from four panels. Its assembly does not require any tools; the panels can be connected as a puzzle. They also differ in their function: consequently, the Castle can be turned into a puppet theater or a market stall. Under both items a silicone strap is installed for security reasons to prevent slipping.

DESIGNERS: Kattuska (Hungary)
YEAR OF DEVELOPMENT: 2012
MAIN MATERIALS: wood

Design: Kattuska

PHOTOS: ANDREA VÉGH

Miniko Dollhouse

The Miniko Dollhouse is made with non-toxic and food safe materials, and showcases designer looks that will make you want a big one of your own. miniio is a Polish company started by a small group of mums and one crafty dad. The set is six times smaller than real life, and each piece has exceptional attention to detail, highest quality and safety and is hand finished. The Miniko "BIG SET" offers the complete dollhouse experience, including a handmade sofa, an oak coffee table, assorted lamps, a solid oak dining table, four chairs, a double bed, an ottoman divan, and a mirror in oak frame, two wallpapers, rugs, and a bamboo terrace.

DESIGNERS: miniio (Poland)
MAIN MATERIALS: wood, stone, metal

Design: miniio

PHOTOS: COURTESY OF THE DESIGNERS

Children's Indian Tent

This fun Indian tent for children was designed by Nathalie Lété for the French toy maker Vilac. Standing at 170 centimeters tall and with a fun and colorful print on the outside, children will have hours of fun playing cowboys and Indians with this tipi. The designs are reminiscent of American Indian traditional symbols, yet are playful enough for a child's room.

DESIGNERS: Nathalie Lété (France)
PRODUCERS: Vilac
MAIN MATERIALS: canvas, hardwood

PHOTOS: COURTESY OF THE DESIGNERS

Skullcave

Guaranteed to be a hit in every household, the skullcave will have your kids begging for more time to play. The lightweight, portable children's play hut is made of extremely durable Sensaten, usually used in foundations of cemented roads throughout Europe. You can be sure that this hut will stand up to even the most energetic play. It can also be unscrewed and rolled up into a compact cylinder for easy storage or transport.

DESIGNERS: Our Children's Gorilla / Christopher Robin Nordström Pitt (Sweden)
YEAR OF DEVELOPMENT: 2002
MAIN MATERIALS: Sensaten, foam plastic

Design: Our Children's Gorilla

PHOTOS: COURTESY OF THE DESIGNERS

Otto + Vroom

Shaped into the figure eight, Otto (Italian for "eight") is not only comfortable but also incredibly interactive. It contains two cars zooming along it as a racetrack made of felt and a neighborhood of building blocks developing around its contours. It is a car racing toy with a retro feel that will please both children and the aesthetic senses of adults. Coated with yellow blackboard paint, each car can be personalized with the provided piece of chalk. Simply wash the writing away to start again. It is a design that fascinates all ages.

DESIGNERS: Mischa Vos (The Netherlands)
YEAR OF DEVELOPMENT: 2008
MAIN MATERIALS: felt and rubber, wood, metal and plastic

Design: Mischa Vos

PHOTOS: COURTESY OF MVOS

My Design Paintable Boots

The paintable boots design kit allows anyone to decorate their own boots, erase and repaint them as many times as they wish. Aiming to boost creativity and self-expression, the designers developed this kit of tools to create personalized boots, which allow the whole family to enjoy the process of creative design. Since the paint can be erased easily with the erasing pads, the same pair of boots can be custom-designed time and again. The kit contains a pair of boots, six flexible waterproof colors, 32 erasing pads, two paint brushes, one pallet, an instruction book and a holding bag.

INVENTOR: Ran Schilo
DESIGNERS: Einat Ben Ari & Tamir Niv
YEAR OF DEVELOPMENT: 2006, 2007, 2008
MAIN MATERIALS: rubber boots, waterproof colors and erasing pads

PHOTOS: COURTESY OF MY DESIGN INC.

PLAYSAM Toys

As the leading Scandinavian design company in its class, PLAYSAM creates innovative and timeless Swedish wooden toys for the young and young at heart. With each and every toy, they not only strive for physical functionality, but also for an art form that challenges pre-existing artistic concepts and conventions. Take your pick of their exclusive products - from the miniature Saab Keychain Car to the Streamliner series to PLAYSAM's wonderful Rocket. Extraordinarily sleek, these wooden toys made of beech from Germany and Italy, and coated numerous times with certified toxin-free lacquer paint, beg to be touched, handled and played with.

DESIGNERS: PLAYSAM (Sweden)
YEAR OF DEVELOPMENT: 1984
MAIN MATERIALS: wood, plastic, metal

PHOTOS: PLAYSAM / JONAS LINDSTRÖM

Toys for Soul

Toys for Soul are three toys which everyone around the world remembers from their childhood: yoyo, spinner, and hole-stick have a universal appeal across generations. All three games are movement games, which can nevertheless be played while seated. The designer provided them with a uniform minimalist shape made of high-quality natural materials in warm shades of brown. The set is handmade in an Indonesian farming village, following the best sustainable practices in terms of materials and production. They are not only popular among children but also help adults improve their concentration and contemplation as well as recall their childhood and have fun.

DESIGNERS: Singgih Kartono
(Java, Indonesia)
YEAR OF DEVELOPMENT: 2007
MAIN MATERIALS: naturally harvested
mahogany and sonokeling wood (Indian
rosewood)

PHOTOS: COURTESY OF AREAWARE

Tube Toys

Tube Toys are a series of vehicles to assemble where the packaging is also part of the product, considerably reducing the amount of the material discarded after purchase. All the parts needed to build each vehicle are contained in a standard cardboard tube, which doubles as the packaging and becomes the body of the car, fire engine, train or tractor. Each tube has pre-cut slots and holes to place the wheels axes and other components. All the materials used to create the product are also recycled and/or recyclable. The cars are easy to assemble and acknowledge the fact that children often enjoy playing with the packaging as much as with the actual toys.

DESIGNERS: Oscar Diaz (United Kingdom)
YEAR OF DEVELOPMENT: 2012
MAIN MATERIALS: cardboard, rubber, bamboo, lowdensity polyethylene

**Design:
Oscar Diaz**

PHOTOS: NPW

Viper Tricycle

The Viper tricycle is a complementing model of the Q-int Triker series. The design of the series is defined by racy features, such as the low seating position, broad rear wheels and the handle bar situated below the saddle. The Viper was developed because the market demanded a smaller and different looking product. The big front wheel and broad rear wheels give the Viper more stability, which makes this an appropriate vehicle for smaller children. Since the Triker family is all about experience, the design team did their best in finding the optimal mix of design, producibility, and most of all: a great and unique racing thrill!

DESIGNERS: Van Berlo design team / Marnix Oosterwelder (The Netherlands)
YEAR OF DEVELOPMENT: 1999
MAIN MATERIALS: metal steel frame, plastic seat and parts, rubber hinges

PHOTOS: COURTESY OF Q-INT. B.V.

**Design:
Van Berlo design team / Marnix Oosterwelder**

Illinois Playhouse

The Illinois Playhouse is inspired by the Modern Movement of the 20th century. It's the ideal place for kids to play alone or with friends, to dream, to create and to imagine. The bay windows flood the playhouse with light but curtains can be pulled for shade or privacy. Come rain or shine, there's no need to worry - the birch plywood is water resistant and thermal insulation cools the interior.

PHOTOS: STARP ESTUDI

DESIGNERS: SmartPlayhouse / David Lamolla
YEAR OF DEVELOPMENT: 2010
MAIN MATERIALS: birch plywood

Design: SmartPlayhouse

X-Hus

The X-Hus is easy to assemble, easy to store and fun to play in. A little Norwegian company with two architects and mothers, Christine Petersen and Anne Frøydis Linnerud, came up with the idea of the X-Hus after realizing that a quality product like this did not exist for kids. The simple, attractive birch playhouse is composed of seven pieces of wood and held together by a clever system of wedges that slot in and out in no time. To store the house, simply hang it on two hooks with the prefabricated holes.

DESIGNERS: Studio17 / Christine Petersen and Anne Frøydis Linnerud (Norway)
YEAR OF DEVELOPMENT: 2011
MAIN MATERIALS: plywood, birch wood

Design: Studio17

PHOTOS: BLATHE SHIELDROP

Enzo the Pull-dog

Anne Kieffer and Arnaud Mouriamé have designed a fabulous collection of kids' furniture, home accessories, and toys made out of silkscreen-printed wood. The simple yet unique designs, coupled with their special patterns makes these toys stand out from the crowd. Enzo the pull-dog is a real classic. It is made of mulitplex panels with screen printing on both sides.

Design:
Studio delle Alpi

DESIGNERS: Studio delle Alpi / Anne Kieffer and Arnaud Mouriamé (Luxembourg)
MAIN MATERIALS: plywood

PHOTOS: COURTESY OF THE DESIGNERS

Toideloi Stackhouse

The Toideloi Stackhouse is a modular dollhouse. Kids or parents can change the dollhouse by arranging and stacking the rooms, balconies and roofs into many unique structures. The Stackhouse is made entirely of wood. The walls of the rooms simply slide together. No screws or tools are required. Kids can build something different every day: a house, skyscraper, village or castle. They can play with the wooden dollhouse from four sides and can separate one set into two houses, so they can play together without being in each other's way.

DESIGNERS: Toideloi / Martijn van Tilburg (USA)
YEAR OF DEVELOPMENT: 2010
MAIN MATERIALS: Baltic birch wood

Design: Toideloi

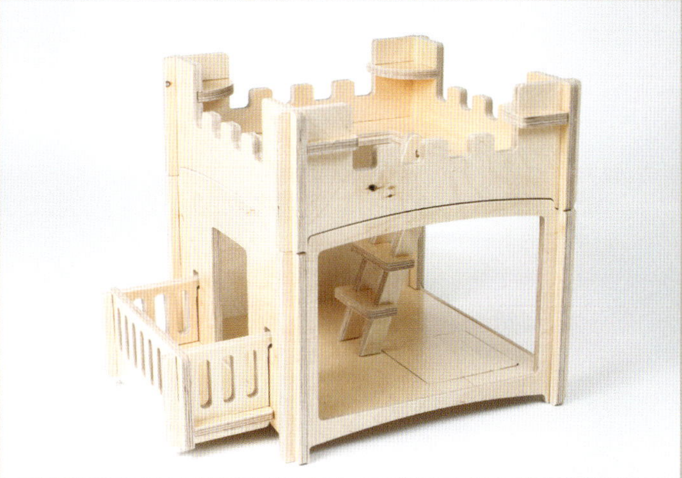

PHOTOS: COURTESY OF THE DESIGNERS

Playhouse

Parents and kids alike will love this eco-friendly playhouse by ZeroEnergy Design. The fun and colorful space offers kids a true retreat, encouraging them to play outside and stay in touch with nature. With a climbing wall, loft area, outdoor chaise, blue racer rocker and chalkboard, your kids will simply never get bored in this haven of play. Storage cubbies offer easy access spaces for toys and games, while crank lights and a crank radio are child-friendly and simple to operate.

Design: ZeroEnergy Design

DESIGNERS: ZeroEnergy Design
YEAR OF DEVELOPMENT: 2012
MAIN MATERIALS: wood and fiber cement

PHOTOS: ROE OSBORN PHOTOGRAPHY

Designers' Index

Imprint

The Deutsche Nationalbibliothek lists this publication in the Deutsche Nationalbibliografie; detailed bibliographic data are available in the Internet at http://dnb.dnb.de

ISBN 978-3-03768-155-8
© 2014 by Braun Publishing AG
www.braun-publishing.ch

The work is copyright protected. Any use outside of the close boundaries of the copyright law, which has not been granted permission by the publisher, is unauthorized and liable for prosecution. This especially applies to duplications, translations, microfilming, and any saving or processing in electronic systems.

1st edition 2014

Editor: Michelle Galindo
Text editing: Judith Vonberg, Michelle Galindo, Lisa Hayek
Layout, graphic concept: Michaela Prinz

All of the information in this volume has been compiled to the best of the editor's knowledge. It is based on the information provided to the publisher by the designers' offices and companies and excludes any liability. The publisher assumes no responsibility for its accuracy or completeness as well as copyright discrepancies and refers to the specified sources (designers' offices). All rights to the photographs are property of the photographer (please refer to the picture credits).